CARLO MARIA MARTINI
BIBLICAL MEDITATIONS

CARLO MARIA MARTINI

ABRAHAM

Our Father In Faith

Published in Australia by
Coventry Press
www.coventrypress.com.au
33 Scoresby Road Bayswater VIC 3153
an imprint of Freedom Publishing Books
www.freedompublishingbooks.com.au

ISBN 9780648323365

English translation copyright © Coventry Press 2019

First published in Italy by Edizioni Borla, Rome 1983

Re-published by
©2016 Edizioni San Paolo s.r.l.
Piazza Soncino 5 – 20092 Cinisello Balsamo (Milano) – ITALIA
www.edizionisanpaolo.it

All rights reserved. Other than for the purposes and subject to the conditions prescribed under the *Copyright Act*, no part of this publication may be reproduced, stored in a retrieval system, or transmitted in any form or by any means, electronic, mechanical, photocopying, recording or otherwise, without the prior permission of the publisher.

Scripture quotations are from the New Revised Standard Version Bible: Anglicised Catholic Edition, copyright © 1989, 1993, 1995 the Division of Christian Education of the National Council of the Churches of Christ in the United States of America.

Catalogue-in-Publication entry is available from the National Library of Australia http://catalogue.nla.gov.au

Printed in Australia by Brougham Press

AN INVITATION	15

PART ONE
MEDITATIONS

Introduction	23
The Title of 'The Spiritual Exercises'	24
'The Exercises' three levels of experience	26
The twentieth introductory observation	28
Abraham, our father in faith	29
But first of all, listen to the word of God	30
Who was Abraham?	33
1. Abraham, our father in faith	34
Abraham is a type for us	34
Abraham is the father of all who seek God	35
Abraham, a father who teaches us the way	35
Our father also in the pilgrimage of faith	37
2. The sources: what do we know of Abraham?	39

	What does the Old Testament say about Abraham?	39
	What does the New Testament say about him?	40
	Judaic and Islamic sources	41
	What do Christian and personal sources say of him?	43
3.	*'Unde?'* What understanding of God was Abraham coming from?	44
	The Book of Wisdom	44
	Seeing God in the stars	46
	When did he come to know God? Three hypotheses	47
	How he came to know God	47
	Our earliest religious experiences	49
	The three possibilities	50
	The 'how' is indicative for us	52
	Values and limitations of a conversion	54
	God's word	56

Abraham's Fears 59

	Abraham's fragility	60
	Our slavery when living with ambiguity	61
1.	Abraham's fear concerning his surroundings	62
	What does Abraham fear?	63
	An ambiguous strategy	65

The powerful instinct for self-defence	66
Yahweh takes pity on poor Abraham	67
Human reaction, God's reaction	69
2. Abraham's fear at home	70
Our shackles; the root of certain disorders	72
A further two examples of this duplicity	73

Gospels for Abraham — 75

What are these gospels?	76
1. Salvation texts	77
Promises made to Abraham	78
Land and descendants	80
Abraham believed in God	82
The Covenant sacrifice	83
What do these texts teach us?	86
2. Three questions to put to Abraham	87
3. The 'gospels" in the Old Testament, and the New Testament Gospel	89
Luke and Matthew give us three texts	90
Proclamations in Paul and Revelations	92
4. The Old Testament Kingdom and the New Testament Kingdom	93
Relationships between these proclamations and the Ignatian 'kingdom'	95

Abraham's social behaviour:
Abraham and social justice — 97

Groans of prayer, groans of creation — 97

1. Abraham divides the land with Lot — 100

    A generous offer — 101

    Abraham's generosity — 102

    Abraham's wealth; the kerygma — 104

    Abraham and the four great kings — 105

    Lot is saved – along with his possessions — 106

    Three reflections — 108

    Abraham shows how truly magnanimous he is — 109

2. The effects of the kerygma on us Christians — 111

    What is the 'treasure' for us? — 112

    Where there is freedom, love can bud forth — 115

    When the word penetrates deeply — 117

Abraham's state of prayer:
prayer, struggle, theology — 119

Abraham, man of few words — 120

Jesus' prayer, Abraham's prayer — 120

1. Prayer of listening — 122

2. Prayer of complaint, lament — 123

    He is provoked by the gap between promise and deeds — 125

    Prayer that could sound blasphemous — 127

3. Prayer of intercession … 128
   The episode with Lot and family at Sodom … 129
   Abraham's 'legal' argument … 131
   Then the negotiation … 132
   The significance of this episode for us … 133
   A sinful group of people … 135
   A God who wants to save by forgiving everyone … 136
   Abraham becomes even more courageous … 138
   A kind of prayer also found in the New Testament … 139

Abraham's test and our trials … 143

1. Abraham's test: analysis of the text … 145
   The four elements of the text … 146
2. Interpretation of the text … 150
   Sarcastic interpretations … 151
   What does the Scripture say? … 153
   The human being faced with limits … 155
   Our tests … 157
   The test that throws our faith into confusion … 158
3. Concluding reflections … 160
   Everyday tests … 160
   The absurdity of certain exceptional tests … 162
   When the test is only a test … 163

Jesus' tests 167
    Three instances of temptation 168
  1. Who are the tempters in the desert? The garden? 169
    Who are the tempters beneath the cross? 171
  2. What is the formal structure of the temptations? 172
    What is the object of the temptations? 173
    The object of the temptation on the cross 175
    A God who does not know how to save 177
  3. How does the victory come about? 177
    The lesson for us: three levels of obedience 179

Abraham's consolation 181
and Christ the consoler 181
  1. Abraham's burial site 182
    The request 184
    The insistence 185
    Negotiations over price 186
    It is sufficient for Abraham to have a small
    plot of land 188
    The guarantee: the Spirit in our hearts 190
    Being buried in Christ 191
  2. Christ our consoler 192
  3. The 'principle and foundation' of Abraham's story 194
    Why God is all in all 196

PART TWO
INSTRUCTIONS

The dynamics of God's word — 201

The dynamics of God's word — 202
A threefold law — 203
Victims of religious alienation — 205
A threat for us Christians too — 207
Looking for Jesus' religiosity — 208

Reform of life, prolonged prayer, penitential spirit and community life — 209

Conquest of self and regulation of one's life — 209
Dealing with inordinate attachments — 210
Persevering in prolonged prayer — 211
'Entering into' prayer: a) the 'confessio laudis' — 213
b) the 'confessio fidei' — 215
Penitential spirit and community life — 216

Qoheleth (the Teacher), Gospel joy, The Rosary — 219

Bitterness, but within a perspective of hope — 220
Jesus is more radically pessimistic — 221
Tolerable limits of pessimism — 223
The Rosary — 225

Like the 'Jesus' prayer	226
The rosary 'reduced'	227

Discernment of spirits 229

Discernment of spirits	229
Evaluation at the level of religious attachment	231
Concerning the emotional resonance of faith	231
To see if they come from grace	232
Two principles for right discernment	234

The *Exercises* and daily life 237

Ultimate and more immediate values	238
An enlightening comparison	239

AN INVITATION

This current volume, dedicated to the figure of Abraham, was published for the first time in 1983. The reflection it contains is developed around three separate paths summed up in the original title of a retreat he was proposing: conquest of self, regulating our life, overcoming inordinate attachments. Three corresponding 'advantages' of Ignatian wisdom are associated with them: solitude, seclusion and 'letting go of' (dismissing, abandoning) the things that divide our attention.

According to Ignatius' teaching, withdrawing from many of our affairs removes the opportunity for nurturing inordinate attachments (the *moral* area, removing what is unacceptable). When the spirit's attention is not divided by many things, the person can then focus on looking for what is truly desired, thus regulating him or herself for one sole purpose (the area of *choice*). Finally, the 'solitary' state of the soul makes it more open to God, nurturing familiarity with the Creator and the capacity to receive his grace and gifts (the *transcendent* area, which opens up to the experience of reaching out to, almost 'touching' God).

This last-mentioned area coincides with the 'conquest of self', not to be understood in any Promethean sense, almost as a challenge to make a last-ditch effort to overcome our limits and challenges, but as an ability to go beyond the timidity of not believing, hoping or trusting. Self-conquest, Martini writes, is 'overcoming fear, death, disappointment, everything in us that is distrustful, suspicious, isolationist, rancorous; it is opening ourselves to the fullness of God and being bathed by him in the truth of our moral existence, our choices, our best service for the greater glory of God.'

Against the background of this reflection, the model of Abraham as the father of those on the journey faith stands out. He is a symbol of all those who seek God. He is our father not only 'in life as it is lived, in faith considered objectively' but also 'for his radical attitude of faith' that makes him 'an exemplary model of the human being in an attitude of acceptance and availability.' Thus he is our 'father in availability, the father of surrender before God's word,' a difficult, gradual, anguished surrender punctuated by light and darkness.

It cannot be taken for granted that this father in faith had had the most truthful experience of the living God, or that he had had such experience immediately (*Second Meditation*). His knowledge of God had a beginning and followed a torturous path. For example, early on he had been nurtured in a received, traditional religiosity and then experienced the command to depart from an unsatisfying, grey, perhaps even cold religious environment.

His setting out on the journey naturally reminds us of the need to free ourselves of the ambiguity of the kind of 'traditional belief' which often predominates in the Christian upbringing of our families, for which the Cardinal has very pertinent words to say: 'it is not that it is not fundamental, but it is tradition, and the tradition underlying Christianity can also obscure it precisely because it is a "leveler", and so can psychologically hamper our awareness of the power of the gospel. The gospel becomes a name for everything that is said and done.'

At the same time, however, the urgency to 'go forth' is also necessarily something that needs to be closely examined: 'The disadvantage, the limitation, is that of certain conversions where people think the conversion is all their own work, an idea they have achieved, and which has become their plaything, their point of obstinacy – these are the fanatical, obstinate kinds of converts who had to break away and set out to invent their own notion of what it is to be religious. Once done, they preserve it, defend it and in its name fight everyone who does not see things the same way.'

The Abraham we know is also someone who contemplates the stars, and he begins to be fascinated and attracted by this profound and growing sense of adoration of a Mystery. But not even this experience is exempt from ambiguity; it is conquered via a deeper self-understanding, which is why it has the intrinsic limitation of being constrained within the perspective of a relationship which embraces God and the cosmos with a very human outlook based on interpretative categories and filters which are always contingent and partial. Is God not perhaps infinitely more than this? The Patriarch will learn this firsthand by directly listening to and contemplating the unpredictable God in his incredible irruption into history. He will do so by experiencing fears, hesitations, inner blockages (*Third*

Meditation). He will do so by discovering how God's ways are capable of surprising and uprooting us.

Abraham's journey is anything but direct. Like every human being he has his moments; his trust is marked by pauses and restarts because for him too 'there was a need to repeat, clarify, apply, specify; the kerygma for Abraham is fundamentally one' but is diversified in its application to the 'individual circumstances of his life.' This is true in consideration of one fact in particular — there is no precedent for God's action. It is utterly new. Desires, expectations, preconceptions will not help him give a more convinced 'Yes'. God's promise is infinitely greater and even though, in a nutshell, he is responding to a primitive human expectation, he does so by radically transforming it.

> Here is the kerygma for Abraham, the promise, what fills his life and because it is accepted in faith, allows him to leave, journey, wander, even though not possessing what he expects at the time. His heart is filled with the great work of God. It has filled his life and is the principle, the point of reference for all the other stances he takes. It is the unique point which allows us to describe why he acts as he does. Why he is able to do these things. It is because he has already received, in faith, a share in the fullness of God. (*Fourth Meditation*)

There is no other reason why, or rather, all the other reasons are partial, powerless, ineffective as explanations for that leap in the dark (or in the light) that was the choice for this Patriarch chosen by God to believe.

In the name of the promise, Abraham is capable of making very free choices which encourage a 'social justice' marked by availability, greatness of heart, gift (*Fifth Meditation*); 'He has something more within, a treasure in his heart... Abraham has the promise. This promise is a greater treasure to him than anything else and it makes him free, calm, available and ready to give the other the best.'

To return to the dominant theme of the retreat, he is free from control by messy emotions; resentment, fears, greed, narrow-mindedness, niggardliness, envy. He is not caught up in revenge, not through any special merit of some personal self-discipline but because of the richness of the gift he has received. Hence Abraham loves, hopes, believes, prays. And while he can be 'bold-faced, even brazen, petulant and apparently even mercenary in his prayer' it is really because of the word/promise he is guarding; he is 'a man who has thrown his whole life behind the word and lives by it' (*Sixth Meditation*).

Otherwise, how could we understand his most radical leap in his understanding of God which is the sacrifice of Isaac? More generally – and this also closely concerns us – how are we to understand a test of such an ultimate kind? Why is there room for something like this in the process of getting to know God?

The answer is not a simple one. Martini's words suggest one with the discretion of someone who wants to encourage our research rather than provide a final answer:

> Because God is God. He gives himself in faith, through a journey of faith, and this journey of faith

presumes we go beyond a largely mistaken original notion of God, at least in part, therefore one to be corrected and as a consequence this implies a series of crises in our idea of God and of our identity before God. This is a terrible fundamental test. There is a basic reason: God is the God of promise, salvation, free initiative, of the word. We, instead, instinctively want a God of security with clear and evident foundations, a God we know everything about, whom we can foresee so that we can plan our way. The clash between these two things is the test. The test is understanding that God is different from how we had understood him. (*Seventh Meditation*)

We could sum up the message of this meditative journey thus: for Abraham, 'from god to God' – from an assumed, 'domesticated' god to the living God – faith is a journey to be embarked on courageously and with the availability of someone who is searching and is not afraid to find something different and greater.

Giuseppe Mazza

PART ONE
MEDITATIONS

First Meditation
Introduction

Lord Jesus, here present,
we thank you for the glory
of your resurrection;
we thank you for calling us together here,
we thank you because in us you are
perfect praise of the Father.
We thank you because in us you are
justice for our brothers and sisters;
you are the one who in us
continuously heals our injustice,
suspicion, fear.
We thank you, Lord Jesus,
for your great glory
and we offer you this activity of ours,
all that we will consider, do
over these days in your honour,
for you.
We also offer you
our tiredness this evening,
since we are a little tired
from today's events too,
like many other days.

> We are content, Lord,
> to present ourselves to you with this tiredness,
> because it is what we are clothed in every day.

And so, grant that as tired and weary as we are, we may begin this activity of ours in the name of the Father, and of the Son, and of the Holy Spirit. Amen.

I thought that this evening I would offer you some reflections on some of the observations [some translations call them 'annotations', literally from St Ignatius' Spanish] from the Ignatian *Exercises*: the second observation, then something regarding the twentieth, but first of all something about the title of the *Exercises* [21][1] which we find just prior to the *Presupponendum* or Presupposition.

The Title of 'The Spiritual Exercises'

The title is: *Spiritual Exercises which have as their purpose the conquest of self and the regulation of one's life in such a way that no decision is made under the influence of any inordinate attachment.* I have reflected a little on this title and the 'conquest of self' sounded a little odd to me. The other phrase, 'the regulation of one's life' seemed clearer to me, that is, by taking the *Exercises* as a structure for our choice of state, we regulate our life, choosing the state God inspires us to choose, or we clarify and deepen

---

[1] Numbers in square brackets refer to the numbered paragraphs in St Ignatius' *Spiritual Exercises*

our understanding of this choice each time we make the *Exercises*. The third phrase is clear enough: 'in such a way that no decision is made under the influence of any inordinate attachment.' This is a work of clarification and separation of our choices from what disturbs us.

So, there are three elements to this title: 1) self-conquest; 2) regulation of our life; 3) overcoming inordinate attachments. While seeking a better appreciation of what these mean, three items came to mind which we find at the end of the twentieth introductory observation.

In these reflections of mine (I will say it just once), be they on the *Exercises* or the Scriptures, I am not aiming at any literal exegesis of the text – there are much better masters at this than I – but am moving myself somewhat freely away from any literal exegesis to one I would rather call 'structural', asking myself what St Ignatius' texts and the biblical text are saying to me when seen as part of Christian life as a whole. I am freeing myself of the restrictions of pure exegesis of the word, taking the word in its context, comparing it with other contexts, trying to see how it can be revealing of Christian existence.

In doing this, I would like to compare these three elements of self-conquest, regulating one's life, rejecting inordinate attachments, with the three advantages St Ignatius lists in the twentieth introductory observation. The three advantages of solitude, seclusion and letting go of things that divide our attention – just as we are doing this evening – or at least trying to leave them behind and trying to seclude ourselves. These are three very interesting things, because as St Ignatius says:

1. The fact that one withdraws from many not-so-well-ordered occupations, removes the opportunity for inordinate attachments and things that are not appropriate.

2. Since our mind is not engaged in many things, it can use its natural powers to seek what it desires, that is, to regulate our life or choose a state in life.

3. And what is of most interest: when the soul finds itself in 'solitude and seclusion', the more fit it renders itself to approach its Creator and Lord and – in the strongly worded Latin text – be closely united with him, or touch and come to him; so the more we touch and come to him, the more prepared we are to receive graces and gifts.

'The Exercises' three levels of experience

Continuing with my reflection, I find that the three elements of the title could be arranged according to three levels of experience in the *Exercises*.

A first, simple level is the *moral* one; removing inordinate attachments, seeing the things in us that are not appropriate, the negative things in our Christian life, our community, role commitments, work; things that hamper, slow us down, weigh upon us. The first fruits of the *Exercises* are at this moral level.

A second level is that of our *choices*; looking for what is best in my life I not only remove the dust but look for what is best. What is best for me? What is the best way to serve God in my life? What will I now choose, leave behind, in order to provide the best service? This is the level of choice.

A third level, which I would call *transcendent,* is the one we do not see, do not touch, but it is at the root of it all, reaching out to God, knowing him, touching him, feeling him, perceiving him in some mysterious but yet very real way, and opening ourselves to him. This transcendent level, which is not the final one in the sense that we have come to the end, is an initial level which also represents the end – mystical union, the fourth week of the *Exercises* – but which for me means conquering myself. Why conquering myself? What does this 'self-conquest' mean, seen at its root, in its profundity? As divided persons what do we have to conquer? What is the reality in us according to Scripture which contrasts with positive reality and is such that we must conquer it? The fundamental reality in us contrasting with positive reality is our 'timidity', our not believing, not hoping, not being open to believing in God, in others, in things. Self-conquest means believing, hoping, trusting. When a person is open to God, God opens himself to that person and in this openness the person finds both the moral level and the level of experiencing choice.

But the transcendent level is the one that dominates everything, is the beginning, the root, the final point and the framework within which the *Exercises* operate. Conquering self is overcoming fear, death, disappointment, everything in us that is distrustful, suspicious, isolationist, rancorous. It is opening ourselves to God and being bathed by him in the truth of our moral life, our life of choice, our best service for the greater glory of God.

The twentieth introductory observation

This threefold group of levels, this threefold set of fruits of the *Exercises* is how I would see the twentieth introductory observation linked to the title of the *Exercises*. Each one should examine himself to see if the Lord is urging him on to explore the level of ascetic moral qualification, or the level of making key choices for better, more lofty things instead of the easier ones we do within the Church but which are not the best that the Lord is asking of us or not yet at the deeper level of direct faith. This latter is a level we can never measure; none of us knows the amount of faith we have, whether we truly and deeply believe in God, or the point at which we do not believe.

All this can be verified both in our moral experience and our experience of choices. However, the third level is the fundamental one and nothing exists without it. Through all the symbols, the things we do, everything we do in the retreat, we continually touch this deeper lever in ourselves which is our basic, unadorned reality as a person before God. It is the level of victory over self, victory over fear, death, mistrust, so we can open ourselves to the word of God who calls us.

We can refer all this to the question the Jews put to Jesus in John 6:28, 'What must we do to perform the works of God?', and which we should paraphrase as 'What must we do do to achieve this or that in the retreat, to gain improvement in something or other?' Jesus' reply immediately sends us to the transcendent level: 'This is the work of God; that you believe in him whom he has sent.'

From this reflection also come the subjects which I propose to develop, taking Abraham the pilgrim as our companion on the journey: looking for God, touching God – what does that mean for us? How is it verified in us? Hence the title for this retreat will be: Abraham, our father in faith.

Abraham, our father in faith

Tomorrow, we will take a better look at this title. This evening, it is sufficient to just point to it. Abraham, our father in faith; faith firstly as a journey, just as Abraham journeyed in faith, groping to understand the God he thought he knew but whom he knew so little. We too are called to walk in faith. Here I am thinking of applying to Abraham's journey and ours what Vatican II, in its Constitution on the Church, says of Mary in its chapter on Our Lady; *in peregrinatione fidei processit*, she advanced in her pilgrimage of faith (LG 58). Our Lady was on a pilgrimage of faith; so she too advanced in getting to know God more. Let us ask God's help that we too may advance on this pilgrimage.

How do we conquer self? How can we conquer the radical mistrust in us that daily closes us off from God and from others to all that is new and true, to hide away in the ivory towers we have made and feel safe in? How do we conquer all this? With God's word. God's word is what wins the battle of faith in us. Here, I recall the second introductory observation of the *Exercises* which says we have to allow ourselves to be penetrated by the word of

God. The person giving the *Exercises* should not be giving of himself or convincing people, but providing the facts, narrating the facts accurately, the story, *narrare fideliter historiam*, the story we need to apply to ourselves by taking the text and asking ourselves: What is the text saying to us? To me? By internalising it, each of us then allows himself to be conquered by the word. For us, this text will be mainly Genesis, Chapters 12-25, and some others as well, including some from the New Testament which refer to Abraham particularly, such as Romans 4, Galatians 3, Hebrews 11.

It is the proclamation of God's word, the kerygma, that achieves this victory. We conquer ourselves if we allow ourselves to be penetrated by the word as God's word, that is, as the power of the Risen Christ present and at work now in this situation.

And here, I return to the point in the twentieth introductory observation regarding segregation, separation, withdrawal. I would like to specify two aspects of this; not so much the results, the fruits I pointed to, but rather the content. What are we withdrawing from? From many things, but especially from all disturbing thoughts.

But first of all, listen to the word of God

In this regard, I was struck some days ago by the observation made by a master of spiritual life during a course of spiritual exercises. In response to the question asked by someone, who was presenting his difficulties: 'But when I begin the *Exercises* I always have a thought, something that concerns me, something I need to think about which I am trying to resolve', he replied: 'This can often happen to us; we start the *Exercises* with something we are obsessed with, that we are concerned about, something we bring with us, maybe a problem we think we can resolve in the light of God. But really it is not so, because we should first of all allow ourselves be penetrated by God's light. The problem can often be a false one which gets in our way and restricts the whole dimension of listening to the word. The many matters we need to withdraw from are not only occupations that would be incongruous in this situation, but also concerns that might seem important and which discernment finally makes us see as a narrow objective which hinders our true openness to the word. Instead of listening to the word within its own framework we are concerned with its applications, a problem (mine or someone else's) which is not the word.'

I say this to indicate some of the things we are asked to separate ourselves from and vigorously abandon, to cut ourselves off from, even if they are apparently good. But what should we not separate ourselves from? It is important to ask this because St Ignatius warns us about it in the twentieth observation when he reminds us that there is a need to give the 'exercitant' (the retreatant) the possibility of attending the Divine Office and Mass. Clearly we are not to separate ourselves from the word of God which is our constant partner. We are not alone, should not be alone. We are in a more determined contact with the word of God. It is not a time of solitude but one of listening. And just as we do not separate ourselves from the word, nor do we separate ourselves from the Church. We are in the Church, we have an experience of the Church and the Church is represented for us by the people with us. Hence we do not separate ourselves from community experience. Indeed, we should experience it more profoundly.

The ideal would be to have this experience by increasingly involving ourselves in what we would like to do. For example, wanting to sit in the second or third row or not to sit in the circle could mean an instinctive desire not to get too involved. Instead, being in the front row clearly has an external significance. We are involved before others, or involved with others.

It is just an example to show what involvement is. An involvement that leads to us putting ourselves fully before the community who know us, also know our faults and judge us, who accept us, hence we are known and judged and should not act without too much pretence. This can happen in prayer, liturgy, spontaneous prayer, questions, requests, sharing after the Gospel, reflections we think could be important for others as well. These are all small experiences of involvement, a corporate involvement which is real and important because these expressions make for a more profound experience of community.

These are the things I wanted to say this evening, and which I will return to tomorrow.

Second Meditation
Who was Abraham?

Out of the depths I cry to you, O Lord
Lord hear my voice!
let your ears be attentive
to the voice of my supplications!
If you, O Lord, should mark iniquities,
Lord, who could stand?
But there is forgiveness with you,
so that you may be revered.
I wait for the Lord, my soul waits,
and in his word I hope;
my soul waits for the Lord
more than those who watch for the morning.
Psalm 130

We ask you, O Lord,
to seek us out as you sought out Abraham
and for us to desire you as he did;
to await, with trust
the manifestation of your word,
who is Jesus Christ, Our Lord,
crucified for us and risen,
and who lives and reigns for ever and ever,
Amen.

We will need to spend a longer time with the Bible this morning. I need to offer some introductory information which will serve for reflection and reading over these days, before proposing the meditation properly so called.

The introductory information concerns the first two points; the first is an explanation of the retreat title, 'Abraham, our father in faith'; the second is a brief summary of sources from which we draw the knowledge of Abraham we are meditating on. Finally, the third point is the meditation as such, which could be expressed thus: from whence, *unde*, or in other words, from what understanding of God did Abraham start out? We will try to respond to this question in the meditation.

1. Abraham, our father in faith

First point – the title: 'Abraham, our father in faith.' Aside from the preposition, four words we will look at in sequence.

Abraham is a type for us

Who is Abraham? Did he exist? Not exist? We could discuss Abraham's historicity, but what interests us is not so much the historical figure of Abraham, the semi-nomad with his flock, probably, but what the biblical tradition has understood about him and his figure, what God did with him, what has been handed down to us from him. Hence, it is what Abraham represents for all who take part in this figure, because Abraham is not just a figure on his own, but also a 'type'. Abraham represents Israel searching for God, Abraham is the human being seeking God, a multitude, all who are seeking God. He is each of us on the journey seeking God, seeking to conform to his word. Hence we will be taking Abraham not in his individual, historical sense but in a representative, global sense.

Abraham is the father of all who seek God

Abraham, our father. What does 'our' mean? Which community are we talking about by saying 'our'? Clearly, we mean all the Christian community. However, this word 'our' extends to the Jewish community whom we spiritually associate ourselves with when seeking our Abrahamic roots, and the Islamic community as well, which gives huge importance to the figure of Abraham. All seekers of God, then, the entire human community insofar as it seeks God.

Here is what we mean, then, by 'Abraham our father'. We place ourselves at this moment in communion with all men and women, boys, girls, the elderly, the dying, the sick of this world who are seeking God; happy and unhappy people, desperate, hopeful, sinner or righteous. Abraham represents all of us in his journey, and we endeavour to undertake this journey in communion with all these people.

Abraham, a father who teaches us the way

In what sense is Abraham a father? Clearly, he is our father in the sense of Chapter 1 of Matthew, where it says:

'Abraham was the father of Isaac, Isaac (was) the father of Jacob...' Along the entire genealogical line as far as 'Jacob (was) the father of Joseph, the husband of Mary, of whom Jesus was born who is called the Messiah,' in whom, we can add, we are all born. So here is our Abrahamic paternity; Abraham the father of Jesus Christ in whom we are all born. He is our father in faith in this sense, because to the extent we live our lives as believers, we are really, ontologically incorporated into Christ and, as such, children of Abraham. Indeed, as Paul teaches, we are true sons and daughters of Abraham, those in whom the promise has been realised.

So Abraham is really our father, that is, we have a relationship with him, an affinity, likeness, we are his descendants. Just as a son or daughter is able to understand what is in the father's heart, so can we understand Abraham. Going even beyond the biblical words we can ask him: Abraham, what were you thinking? How did you behave? Why did you do this? What was in you? What did you see? It will be a conversation we hold internally, but on the basis of our genealogical affinity with him, as one might speak with one's deceased father: Why did you do this? How would you have looked at this?

Our link with Abraham as father is not only in the genealogical sense. It is also by way of example. In fact, when the liturgy speaks of 'our father in faith' it is saying that Abraham goes before us as a true father, teaches us the way, gives us the tradition, points out how we should conduct ourselves. Hence the events, fears, solitary moments, and the grace of Abraham are a sign, symbol, example of the events, fears, solitary moments and graces of all human beings and of each of us before God. Abraham our exemplary father is what makes these meditations of ours on the Old Testament possible, because in him our own destiny is also at play and he is an example of this destiny of ours before the word, before God.

Our father also in the pilgrimage of faith

Our father *in faith,* the final words of the title. We already hinted at it yesterday; this faith has several meanings, including an objective, content-based one. Abraham is our father because he is the ancestor of this religiosity, this way of expressing our faith. Our religiosity is Abrahamic, just as Islam's and Judaism's is Abrahamic. They are special characteristics of this Abrahamic faith. He is our father not only in life as it is lived, in faith considered objectively, as an overall experience of faith, but also, as moderns always highlight, he is principally our father for his act of faith, for his radical attitude of faith. He is the exemplary model of the human being in an attitude of acceptance and availability. In this sense, he is our father in availability and openness of faith and hope.

Here, we could paraphrase the words of the *Exercises* in the part known as the Principle and Foundation: 'Therefore, we must make ourselves indifferent to all created things,' saying 'Therefore, we should be like Abraham. Abraham presents himself to us as the father of indifference, the father of availability, the father of surrender before God's word. It is a difficult gradual, anguished surrender, as we will see, but it is precisely this surrender, this acceptance of the word, this believing and hoping against all hope that justifies Abraham according to Paul. Hence, he is our father in this radical, fundamental act of our Christian life which is, as Vatican Council II says in the Constitution on Divine Revelation; 'the act by which man entrusts himself to God totally, freely' (no. 5).

But as well as being our father in religiosity and the act of faith, Abraham is also our father in the journey of faith, which we mentioned yesterday when speaking of Our Lady: '*Maria in peregrinatione fidei processit.*' Abraham also advanced in faith and we can meditate on Abraham's life as a pilgrimage of faith. Even though it is a personal idea of mine, I see here a possible link with the retreat.

Abraham's life is a pilgrimage of faith from a certain point of departure to a certain point of arrival, passing through specific stages. What are the *Exercises*? A journey, a 'pilgrimage' from a certain point of departure to a point of arrival, with specific stages which outwardly are four weeks, and more pointedly, the four or five fundamental meditations. In the *Exercises*, too, there is a story, a journey; there is progress, there are stages marking this story. Now if you read the thirteen chapters given to Abraham in Genesis, you will see that these chapters are presented as a unity, a pilgrimage, a story, with a degree of gradualness, stages, basic meditations.

It seems to me, then, that we can meditate on Abraham's journey, maintaining for ourselves the gradual rhythm of the weeks of the *Exercises*, following Abraham as our father on this journey too, the journey of faith. It is interesting how all the exegetes see Abraham's story as a unified cycle arranged according to a gradual perspective. So, we are also in line with what the exegetes say if we try to enter into Abraham's heart, entrusting ourselves to this consonance of feeling with him. This is what I have to say concerning the title of our retreat.

2. The sources: what do we know of Abraham?

Second point: the sources. What will help us as we meditate on Abraham? Yesterday, I already cited the principle sources: Genesis 12-25, and from the New Testament especially Romans 4, Galatians 3, Hebrews 11. Nevertheless, it is good to take a broader look at sources, especially since we have more time over these days and you can organise meditations and reading a little more extensively on your own. We could mention many sources on Abraham. I will mention five, five groups of sources we will dip into quite literally. They are very rich sources from which we will take bits and pieces.

Firstly, there are the biblical sources, not only Genesis 12-25, but some other passages from the Old and New Testaments.

What does the Old Testament say about Abraham?

We find the name stated as 'Abram' 60 times in the Old Testament and 174 times in the form 'Abraham', so more than 230 mentions all up. We find the latter 72 times in the

New Testament; a total of 306 mentions. Yet the books of the Old Testament which mention Abraham are fewer than one might think; the figure of Abraham is not so popular in the Old Testament. It is later Judaism, in my view, which highlights him. The ancient wisdom tradition hardly dealt with him, never mentions the name Abraham. In the more recent deutero-canonical wisdom tradition he is to be found in Wisdom and Ecclesiasticus

There is a brief passage about him in the Book of Wisdom, and in Ecclesiasticus he is spoken of in the 'praises of the Fathers.' Only two psalms mention Abraham: Psalm 47 and 105. We find seven mentions in the Prophets but relatively few, really, and more in the later prophetic books. Probably because early prophetism is not inspired by Abraham to the extent that some of the later prophets were. There are also 18 mentions in the Pentateuch other than in Genesis: Leviticus and Deuteronomy. Abraham's name recurs fairly often in the formula 'the God of Abraham', which tells us nothing about him. He is mentioned 15 times in the historical books, once in Maccabees. One could say that the figure of Abraham took on greater importance in the Bible beginning with the Exile (Exodus).

What does the New Testament say about him?

Abraham is mentioned 72 times in the New Testament – followed immediately by the Koran which mentions him 69 times – compared with 80 mentions of Moses. Abraham and Moses are the two most mentioned personalities in the New

Testament. Fewer mentions are made of Jacob (25 times), Isaac (20 times), and other minor figures in Abraham's story: Hagar 2 times, Esau 3 times and Rachel and Rebecca once. Sarah is mentioned 4 times.

Among the mentions of Abraham in the New Testament books I think the two Canticles are important: the *Magnificat*, 'according to the promise he made to our ancestors, to Abraham and to his descendants forever' (Lk 1:55), and the *Benedictus:* '(and has remembered)... the oath that he swore to our ancestor Abraham' (Lk 1:73).

These are important because we recite them daily in the Breviary, morning and evening, recalling Abraham in our priestly prayer. Another important passage which is indicative of Abraham is John 8:58: 'before Abraham was, I am.' And there are other passages.

These are the biblical texts you could take a look at yourself and, as St Ignatius tells us, you will discover much more joy, be able to savour them better than just by listening to them.

Judaic and Islamic sources

There are a number of Judaic sources on Abraham and, in my opinion, very important ones for the very same reason we are meditating on Abraham here. The Jews, especially beginning with the Exile and beyond, reflected much on Abraham: Who was he? What did he do? What did he think? What did he want? Clearly, they do not have the historical value of tradition but they do have value for a religious interpretation of the figure of Abraham. They were people who felt he was close to them and they almost had him speaking to them. They are first-rate documents even if, as we shall see, at times a little simplistic, even puerile. Yet, even in this apparent puerility the Rabbis said some amazing things. They had the art of saying some profound things with a tiny little detail, a brief tale, a small hypothesis simply floated, and they said things that make us reflect.

There are two sources from Hellenistic Judaism: Philo, who has many passages on Abraham, and Josephus Flavius, who tells the whole story of Abraham in his own way in his *Antiquities of the Jews*. We can read with interest in these sources how the author portrayed Abraham, doing what we are doing here and will do: trying to understand Abraham in the context of his own religious circumstances. Clearly, this would be mistaken if we were to attribute historical value to it, but becomes legitimate if given religious value by asking what Abraham might be saying to me now, seeing myself as Abraham! This is what Philo does, interpreting Abraham from his religious viewpoint, Josephus Flavius does it and in much more fragmentary form but perhaps more discerningly. And the sources of rabbinical Judaism do so too: the Haggadah, the rabbinical accounts of Abraham's infancy and his various adventures.

Islamic sources, as I have indicated, are quite numerous. Islam has great feeling for the figure of Abraham. There are some very beautiful texts, some of which we will sample if we have time.

What do Christian and personal sources say of him?

Finally, we have *Christian* sources, all the Christian reflection on Abraham. First of all there is the Patristic reflection. While it hasn't provided whole tracts on him as it did for Moses – the *Life of Moses*, by Gregory of Nyssa – he certainly abounds in mention.

Other than the Fathers, there is all the spiritual reflection in liturgy, Christian art, iconography, novels, modern portrayal, all that the Christian vein of thought has reflected on while trying to understand itself in the light of this figure. It is enough to mention, for example, the famous paintings by Rembrandt, four I think, of various moments in Abraham's life where the artist attempts to interpret in various ways what would have happened in those moments. What Abraham is saying to the religious conscience, etc.

The final source is personal: me as Abraham, how I will see him as part of my journey, obviously without pretending to give any historical or exegetical value to it, but as a Christian interpretation. This is very important, because each of us has had and will have an experience of Abraham and so can read the pages that deal with him by referring to personal experience. So, those listed above are some of the sources I would indicate to you to consider.

3. '*Unde?*' What understanding of God was Abraham coming from?

The third point: we have arrived at what will be the first meditation for today, where we enter what is the First Week of the *Exercises* practically speaking – I will explain this better in the evening instruction.

Yesterday evening, recalling the 'Principle and Foundation', I made some reference to the aim we are proposing, the level we want to be at, what we want to gain. We are now directly entering into the *Exercises* with some meditations, one today, another tomorrow, which will help our self-awareness through the mirror of Abraham.

The theme of the meditation is this: *Unde?* Or in other words, specifying more clearly what knowledge, what understanding of God Abraham was coming from. This theme could have a sub-theme which I would express thus: 'The values and limitations of our early religious experience.' We too have a departure point in our religious life, just as Abraham did. And just as we can meditate on the eternal King by meditating on an earthly king, so too when it comes to meditation on the Kingdom by contemplating the departure point for Abraham's religiosity, we will be reflecting on our own departure point in our journey to God.

The Book of Wisdom

What understanding of God did Abraham begin with? It is difficult to know, because the Bible does not say, does not recount who Abraham was before his call in Genesis 12.

We can speculate on something of Abraham's starting point for his religious journey from Wisdom 10:5, where it speaks about Abraham without actually naming him, in words that are somewhat enigmatic; 'when the nations in wicked agreement had been put to confusion, [Wisdom] recognised the righteous man and preserved him blameless before God, and kept him strong in the face of his compassion for his child.' Although some of this refers to Abraham after the call, what we can draw from the text is that Abraham's religiosity emerged from an experience of confusion and wickedness, in continuity with Genesis 14:22.

This is quite a mysterious chapter from the point of view of literary criticism as well. All the critics set it aside; it is not part of the Yahwist, Elohist or Priestly sources. It is a source all of its own – we do not know where it comes from, but certainly it contains extremely ancient data. Discoveries at Ebla have shown that the names of the five cities mentioned in Genesis 14:2, 'these kings made war with King Bera of Sodom, King Birsha of Gomorrah, King Shinab of Admah, King Shemeber of Zeboiim, and the king of Bela (that is, Zoar)', names about which nothing was known were discovered on a tablet at Ebla from 2,300 years before Christ. That means that a link between the five cities already existed before the Bible was written. The Bible here is recalling traditions that have disappeared from the common memory, names people could not verify.

Seeing God in the stars

In Genesis 14:22, we have what Abraham tells the king of Sodom: 'I have sworn to the LORD, God Most High, maker of heaven and earth.' Usually, Abraham does not speak this way. Here is Abraham before the one God contemplated from the perspective of the splendour of creation, and I believe this reveals a primitive religious experience faced with the majesty of creation, an experience probably prior to the word of God coming to him. I say this because the rabbinical sources invite me to say it. We should not wonder at the fact that Abraham speaks of a Most High God, creator of heaven and earth. Abraham came from a place where astrology was very much cultivated, so he had to have this very profound sense of the heavens. In fact, when God does speak to him, one of the comparisons he uses is that of the stars: 'Look toward heaven and count the stars, if you are able to count them... So shall your descendants be.' The invocation of the God of Heaven seems bound up with a religious experience from an earlier period.

There would be archaeological sources we could mention. Scholars have racked their brains for decades over the religious environment Abraham was born into: polytheism, the worship of El, of multiple divinities, or the worship of the One God in Mesopotamia? There could be many a hypothesis, a theory, but we can only discover what Wisdom tells us: he came from a wicked, corrupt and difficult religious environment. I think we can say that much and furthermore, archaeology and history confirm it.

When did he come to know God? Three hypotheses

I refer here to the rabbinical sources which attempt to enter into Abraham's heart; they are not reasoning from generic, uncertain data, but trying to get inside him. I found these sources mentioned in a very interesting book by Robert Martin-Achand: '*Actualité d'Abraham*'. It is interesting because it is a collection of the most ancient texts on Abraham. The author provides a summary of rabbinical sources: 'As regards the rabbinical sources there are various ideas, various hypotheses. According to some, Abraham knew God when he was one year old, having received a special grace, and came to know God. According to others he was three when he came to know God and then began to be educated, brought up in the religion of Seth and Noah. Others say he came to know God after a lengthy pilgrimage from error to error when he was 48 years old.'

I don't know where this '48 years old' came from, and not even the Rabbis agree among themselves. Why do they mention these three ages 1, 3, 48 and not others? What were they trying to say? We call this the 'when' question.

How he came to know God

The Rabbis not only asked themselves about the 'when' of Abraham coming to know God, but also the 'how', and here too there are many ideas. According to some, the 'how', if he was only 1, happened through an extraordinary revelation, like the early conversions of St Ignatius when

God enlightened him in an extraordinary way. In this case we have nothing to add.

But if we go further on in age, then the 'how' can be family upbringing, personal reflection. Philo, from Hellenic Judaism, offers the following idea in his *Treatise on Virtues*: Abraham was a Chaldean and lived in a setting given to astrology, from which he drew the notion of a god who was One, the beginning of everything, not generated, creator of the universe; and so gradually he arrived at the notion of the One God.

He gives other clarifications in his *Book of Jubilees*, where he recounts some details of Abraham's experience at 14 years of age, when he discovers man's corruption, and separates from his father to avoid worshipping false gods. He unsuccessfully attempts to convince his father not to worship idols, then decides to burn the idols, while his brother, wanting to save them from the fire, dies in the flames. The idea of flames arises because at a certain point in the Bible God says to Abraham: 'I am the God who rescued you from the flames of the Chaldeans.' The Rabbis asked themselves: What are these flames? Perhaps a fire where everyone was about to perish? Or the corruption of the Chaldeans which God saved him from?

Abraham asks God to help him not to fall back into error, to point out everything he must do, and then comes the voice of God, so Abraham had to have had contact with God, a sense of God which allowed him to turn to him and listen to his voice. Therefore, some Rabbis say that this sense of God would have come to Abraham from the family who brought him up. Others say, instead, that he rebelled against his father, an astrologer. Still others say that by looking at the starry sky, the heavens, he had a profound religious experience (which is why I quoted Genesis 14:22; cf. also 15:5 ff.).

According to this last mentioned group of Rabbis, by looking at the star-spangled sky, Abraham came to clearly understand that it was not the stars which had to be served but the master of the stars, the One who made them. It is a natural kind of religious experience we would say, one of transcendence, causality, the limits of things which opened him to a sense of God.

Yet another hypothesis could be put forward according to some, probably those who plumped for 48 years of age, and it is this: Abraham probably experienced a kind of peaceful idolatry, a generic sense of God, but God's word converted him. Hence his knowledge of God, his true knowledge of God, came about at the moment of the call. Here, conversion and call are identical.

Our earliest religious experiences

Now, reflecting on these things, I asked myself: What did the Rabbis do? All they did was to multiply the number of Abrahams according to the various possibilities of human existence, and described most of them. This is why, while putting together the reflection on the 'when' and the 'how', I wanted to invite you and me to follow this whole canvas provided by the Rabbis: 'When?' At 1, 3, 48? 'How?' In the family or against his family and environment? Through inner religious experience? Through God's word, a gospel?

They are all important possibilities, each of which – and here is the sub-theme of the third point – has its values and limitations. It is important for us to examine the values and limitations of our earliest religious experience which we clearly carry with us through life, the first way we began approaching God which might have lasted years, decades even. We should consider it in relationship to the world which gives primacy to the word, the gospel approach. This could preserve leftovers, often quite strong ones, from our earliest experiences, which is why it is important to examine ourselves.

The three possibilities

Let us take the three rabbinical ages in their symbolic sense: 1, 3, 48 years of age. What does 1 year of age want to say? This is the earliest that God can immediately reveal himself to the soul in fullness and clarity. As with Our Lady, certain privileged individuals, perhaps some of us, had this from the very outset. It is an infused understanding of God, a truly profound one, rooted within one, clearly a grace, a huge grace, and a very rare one.

3 years of age: What could this be saying? In the family, the family teaching the first prayers and God's name; becoming accustomed to religious symbols, like the sign of the cross and the crucifix. This is the family upbringing of a normal kind, I would say, which many of us would have

known. Being born into a family such that without any special predispositions – as St Stanislaus, St Aloysius tell us – it leads us to accept these signs and symbols and make them our own, and brings us into a community of prayer, to a church, beside our mother, our parents, seeing them pray, go to communion. This is the beginning of a profound religious process.

48 years of age? What does this say? This is the more difficult, often deviant path which passes through all the possible aberrations of thought, wandering a bit here and there, like St Augustine, looking to right and left. Perhaps at this point we can thank God if he has given us an initial infused experience, and we must thank him for the whole process of coming to maturity in the family he has given us. However, we should also put the question to ourselves: is it possible that it would take forty eight years before coming to know the true God? Yet this happens, at least at certain levels, even in the Christian world.

I was struck some time ago by what I heard a priest say about helping out with a Neocatechumenal catechesis, and he came to the bishop all surprised, saying: 'Finally I have understood the kerygma!' The bishop asked: 'Is that possible? You, who have been preaching it in church for many years and teaching it at the seminary?' I am saying that one can actually spend many years in a generic religious experience without having any deep understanding of it, remaining somewhat outside it, almost like an atheist. And I believe this is more common than we think, a religious experience that never goes in-depth. It is not to say it is bad. It just is, and God calls us later, God waits till later. It is just as certain that the means by which we achieve a truly religious experience, the purification of an earlier experience, are many and unpredictable, have no specific time and can last for decades. Hence the importance of asking ourselves: What were the beginnings? What was the 'when'? Try to identify the time, these years, this period, or that prolonged difficulty, this light and shade with trials of desolation, God's absence, 'there is no God!', and then the recovery. We should recall all of this briefly, put it before God, and think of Abraham's original experience.

The 'how' is indicative for us

But even more than the 'when', the 'how' is of interest and it is on the 'how' that I am really inviting you to meditate because it is important, not only because we are driven by the values and curbed by the limitations of the 'how' of our early religious experiences and others that followed, but also because they are itinerant experiences that need to be purified.

We can look at this 'how' according to the four possibilities proposed by the Rabbis: 1) family upbringing in the tradition of Seth and Noah; 2) the need to detach himself from his pagan family; 3) looking to the stars in the heavens; 4) listening to God's word.

The first is experience in the family, continuing an ancient tradition. We all know the immense value of this type of religious upbringing. Christianity is a tradition, not a religion bereft of one. We are inserted into a living tradition. It is an immense grace to be born into, brought up in a Christian tradition. But we also know the limitations of this traditional Christianity, the fact that so many things, once received, have become ordinary, evident, obvious to the point of no longer standing out for us, just like the priest who knew how to preach the kerygma very well, knew his Vatican II, the Paschal Mystery, Christ who died and rose, but had not given prominence to this experience of his. Christianity embraced everything: Christian democracy, frequent communion, confession, liturgy, church duties, all a laborious complex of things to be done; the priest could spell out the kerygma with his lips and his mind too, but he had not grasped in any fundamental way the power that the evangelical word of death and resurrection has to dominate and change the entire panorama of religious tradition. One that comes to us like a river and hence without differences, or highlights, or clarity between its central and peripheral points.

It is the great difficulty of a religious tradition received like a great treasure in which everything is to be observed, done well. Where everything is important, valid, and to be defended. However, it is a treasure which becomes a burden, ambiguous at a certain point, and hinders our understanding of God. It could well be that up until 48 years of age, someone has no real knowledge of God because of this energy-sapping baggage behind it all. There is no possibility of a pristine, clear understanding of the core of the mystery.

Here, then, is the ambiguity of the Christian tradition. It is not that it is not fundamental, but it is tradition, and the tradition underlying Christianity can at the same time also obscure it precisely because it is a 'leveler', and so, psychologically can hamper our awareness of the power of the gospel. The gospel becomes a name for everything that is said and done. This is our first experience.

Values and limitations of a conversion

The second experience: detachment from family, the need to soon exit a mediocre, grey, contrary, atheistic or agnostic, indifferent religious experience which is of no help. It is an experience with the notable advantage of greater personalisation, greater clarity of personality. The disadvantage, the limitation, is that of certain conversions where people think the conversion is all their own work, an idea they have achieved, and which has become their plaything, their point of obstinacy – these are the fanatical, obstinate kinds of converts who had to break away and set out to invent their own notion of what it is to be religious. Once done, they preserve it, defend it and in its name fight everyone who does not see things the same way.

Here, too, we see the same phenomenon: what is advantageous is also ambiguous; it can be a selfish, possessive kind of religiosity, a strong but limited one. They have grasped one idea and that idea has embraced everything, become an ideology they want to advance at any cost. How much we have suffered from enduring ideologies that people around us have sought to impose on us! Each one wants to convince the other of his or her ideology because it is his or her conquest, a precious treasure to be foisted on others at any cost. This is the limitation that goes with the advantage of personalisation, of the richness of religious enthusiasm. The limitations are visible not only in the annoyance these things can be for others but also in the aberrations that often follow, parabolas of great success that end up with a mighty fall.

The third experience: Abraham's poetic, romantic experiences looking at the stars. A simple man, he lived in a peaceful environment, one of astrology, but not of the fanatical kind as something quite evident. He surveys the stars and feels there is something more, that astrology does not suffice – there has to be something commanding these things, someone who has them in hand. A sense of profound and luminous adoration before a mystery is born in his heart, the *mysterium tremendum* that fascinates, the One who is different, Other, Absolute. So, he gradually arrives at this natural, profound, very rich religious experience which has enormous advantages because it is personal, experienced inwardly, is tied to a cosmic experience capable of guiding his life.

Is this experience also an ambiguous one? Yes, for sure, because it is a religious experience won through coming to a deeper self-understanding, hence limited to a relationship between God and the cosmos that comes from this perspective. It is true that whoever has arrived at this metaphysical concept could also take some distance from it and conceive of God's freedom in a full and complete way, but it seems to me it is always a certain way of looking at God in relation to one's own experience. It is a religious experience that, at a certain point, can become a veil, an obstacle, even a dam blocking God's word because we are already satisfied with our own perspectives and they seem to be sufficient. It can be a vague, generic religiosity, an intellectual, confident kind of theism, which for that very reason can end up masquerading as God's word. We all carry something of this with us – our religiosity is a mixture of these profound experiences of ours which are not yet really converted, clarified; they have not yet escaped the ambiguity of God's word.

God's word

Finally, the only real, truly valid and definitive experience: Abraham converted by the experience of the word. This is when he understands that God is the Absolute, the Different one, the Luminous one, the Fascinating one who speaks, acts freely, breaks into his life the way He wants to, not as Abraham imagines it to be, not according to some cosmic measure but in an unpredictable, unknowable way because God is the unknowable, the unknowable who acts. As we shall see, a completely new tumult arises in Abraham's soul.

I believe that this last experience can be glimpsed – as many say, basing themselves on archaeology and some interpretations of the ancient texts – in the shift Abraham makes from El to Yahweh. El: the great and peaceful God of the firmament who holds all beneath him, controls the course of things, the seasons, the stars, to whom we adjust and who adjusts to us, to our pastoral, agricultural rhythms – hence a natural, simple religiosity. Yahweh: the God, a tribal God as some of the Ebla descriptions would have us believe, a God who comes down from the mountain to speak with violence, in a rush, gets involved, joins the fight, changes things, demands, yet at the same time is mysterious, the Most High, the Absolute, the Inaccessible.

This shift in Abraham will mark the rhythm of his whole life and will constantly trip him up as we shall see. But, it is openness to the word, the unpredictable, unknowable word in the source from which he comes, because we do not know God, have never seen him, do not know who he is. Yet, we know he acts within us and we trust him, without knowing him deeply, involved as we are in this journey.

It is the experience of conversion which is also a call, a vocation, the experience Abraham eventually had but which always needs to be improved and repeated.

And we? Have we had this experience? And if so, when was it repeated? How did it happen? What is it like now? How do I find myself before the mystery of God now?

There are many ways this could happen: understanding, rejection, negligence, ambiguous adherence, even clearer adherence. These are all possible approaches in religious life too – and especially in religious life I believe, in which everything that separates human beings from God emerges much more. Hatred of God, contempt, rejection, inability to recognise him, resentment. All those attitudes emerge much more strongly because God becomes the partner in our life and this sets up our struggle with God.

It is important to recognise this struggle in us, just as there was a struggle in Abraham, and to let it emerge before the mystery of the word. So let us repeat this search Abraham made for God by reciting some lines from Psalm 119:

> Let my cry come before you, O LORD;
> give me understanding according to your word.
>
> Let my supplication come before you;
> deliver me according to your promise.

THIRD MEDITATION
Abraham's Fears

In the chapter of Genesis where it speaks of Abraham, we find some fifteen or so episodes, five of which can be considered fundamental for his relationship with God. They are as follows; the call, Chapter 12 (Yahwist); the promise and Covenant, Chapter 15 (with Elohist traits); the new Covenant and Abraham's circumcision at 99 years of age, Chapter 17; the episode with Sodom and the power of Abraham's prayer, Chapter 18; finally, the sacrifice of Isaac, Chapter 22. It seems to me these are five rather large episodes but very interesting ones, even if others are no less significant.

This morning, however, I propose to speak of three, let's say minor, episodes: Abraham and the Egyptians, Chapter 12:10-20; Abraham at Gerar, Chapter 20:1-18 (which is a duplicate of the preceding one and we will tackle it separately); Abraham's family problem with Sarah and Hagar, Chapter 16:1-16. Three episodes reduced to two: first, Abraham's fear at what surrounds him; second, Abraham's fear regarding his family's survival. We will bring these two episodes together under a single title: 'Abraham's fears', meditating on them along the lines of the First Week of the *Exercises*, investigating what there is in the human being who find himself in the presence of God's word.

Abraham's fragility

In contrast to yesterday, when we were grasping at straws a bit with the Rabbis and the Haggadah in the effort to understand what was going on with Abraham in Ur of the Chaldeans, here we can follow the biblical text instead. Abraham is already attentive to the promises, so *a fortiori* he is already open to the kerygma and the revelations of God's word to follow. But in fact, he receives them only in part and so only partially benefits from his growing understanding of God. He does not spread the word sufficiently, it gets blocked in him sometimes, and hence Abraham's fragility emerges.

This fragility of Abraham's, as we shall see, is subtle. It dabbles in ambiguity and that is why it is useful for us. Ordinarily, human weakness is easy to recognise and admit when expressed as serious sinfulness – those who kill, steal etc. But when it is more subtle, more ambiguous, then it is much more difficult to perceive.

This is what St Ignatius asks us to explore in the three colloquies which follow the repetition of the second meditation on sins, in which I ask that I may understand the disorder of my actions so I can put my life back into order; that I may know the world's vanity in order to be horrified by it. The graces requested go beyond knowledge of our sins to an understanding of what is less orderly in my life, what is under pressure, involves compromise, subtle deception. These things are a part of life for someone who does not walk fully in the light of the word, who is not yet fully involved in the promise.

Our slavery when living with ambiguity

To further clarify this idea, let us meditate on the two episodes as well as remind ourselves of the Ignatian texts of the penitential prayer, the three colloquies, also seeing these in the light of Hebrews 2:14-15, another important text for understanding human frailty: 'Since, therefore, the children share flesh and blood, he himself likewise shared the same things, so that through death he might destroy the one who has the power of death, that is, the devil, and free those who all their lives were held in slavery by the fear of death.'

This text is a brilliant interpretation of the slavery of the human being who lives with ambiguity as a victim of worldly forces which are the forces of the environment, public opinion, what others expect of us, things we fear being criticised for or being seen in a bad light for, and for which we must be ignored, counted as of little worth. This is the kind of slavery, St Paul says, which is the fear of death in its broadest sense, meaning the fear of diminishment, of being split, lost, of cutting a poor figure, no longer being part of the mainstream, being tossed aside.

This fear, in reference to the final moment which is death, or our disappearance from the context of life, underpins all the anxieties of the human being in his or her daily struggle, and hence is the origin of all the other conflict in which human beings attempt to prevail, resist being set aside, and, in fact, do the same to others by riding roughshod over them. They are trying not to be caught out, attempting to find a secure path. All of this reality is picked up in

Hebrews 2:14-15, and we can read, in all its simplicity, how this reality turns up in the two episodes involving Abraham.

1. Abraham's fear concerning his surroundings

The first episode, as I said, is duplicated. Be it in Egypt or at Gerar, Abraham keeps quiet about his wife's true identity and in Egypt presents her as his sister and acts such that she will be considered this way. It should be noted that in Genesis 26, Isaac will do the same. I asked myself, why the insistence on this detail recounted three times? Whenever the Bible tells us something three times there is a reason for it. Paul's call is recounted three times, Jesus predicts his passion and death three times, so there has to be a reason.

It is not just a simple little detail, as some commentators maintain, including the Jerusalem Bible, which says that basically it is a little story to make us look upon the beauty of Jewish women as one of the glories of that race, and even older women were beautiful enough to be desired by foreigners; or that the Bedouin were very smart, and while being devoid of any great power, they were able to get by through acts of shrewdness.

All of this might have been the basis of the original account, the kind of story told in the tents which people laughed and joked about. But in real terms, once it was introduced into the Abraham cycle of stories, and mentioned three times, it seems to have taken on moral significance even if, as we shall see, it is not the one we might immediately expect. In the context of Genesis 12 it seems to me that it really means that Abraham was not yet able to fully benefit from the growing understanding of God given to him, but is quickly caught up in old fears, old ways of self-preservation, by getting around things and situations.

This is how I suggest we interpret the duplicated episode: first, by looking at the context, the structure in a brief textual analysis, then by asking some questions: What was Abraham afraid of? What does he do when driven by fear? What does Yahweh do? Then two additional questions concerning ourselves: What does the man Abraham fear? How is he a type of the human being in difficult situations, ones that worry us, are a bit risky. What does he feel? What does he do? How does God look on this man? These are the three important points in the text, I feel, for understanding the episode we are looking at.

But first of all, a brief analysis of the context and structure.

What does Abraham fear?

The context is most significant in that it immediately follows on from the magnificent promise in Genesis 12:3; it is a marvelous promise which says among other things: 'I will bless those who bless you and the one who curses you I will curse.' So, Abraham can rest assured and consider that God will defend him. Abraham partly obeys and has a new vision of the future. In the following verses it says that he calls on God, builds him an altar, and all is magnificent. And then in verse 10, Abraham finds himself in Egypt midst problems, his own difficulties and he reacts as best he can. This is the context.

Briefly, how can we structure 12:10-20? In 20:1-18 we have an Elohist document, a richer, more elaborate account and a more structurally complex one, but it has the basic structure of the simpler account in 12:10-20.

First element, the occasion for this situation, is a famine. Abraham goes down to Egypt 'because there was a famine in the land,' a circumstance, as we know, that would be repeated in Joseph's time. It is one of the constants in this flow from Palestine to Egypt.

Second element, verses 11-13: fear. Abraham tells Sarah: 'When the Egyptians see you, they will say, "This is his wife"; then they will kill me.' Abraham is afraid of dying, hence the strategy: 'Say you are my sister so that it may go well with me because of you, and that my life may be spared on your account.' He is even hoping for some advantage, to gain something from life's struggle there, and not only be safe but increase in wealth.

The same fear and strategy more or less apply in Chapter 20:1-18 where they are expressed a bit more elaborately as we see in verse 11. Abraham says: 'I did it because I thought, there is no fear of God at all in this place, and they will kill me because of my wife.' Here is the religious motivation: they do not fear God, so I need to think of myself. I have to defend myself. Abraham also thinks of saving face when he says: 'Besides, she is indeed my sister, the daughter of my father but not the daughter of my mother, and she became my wife.' This is the Elohist tradition which seeks to place

Abraham in a better light: she is truly his sister, Abraham had good reason for speaking this way.

The Yahwist tradition in Chapter 12 does not provide details, so there can only be hypotheses, none of them definite. Some refer to a Mesopotamian custom. According to others there would be a justification inasmuch as he could truly declare his wife by elevating her to the rank of sister, a special rank, probably to give her special dignity compared to his other wives, as a person he had acquired not from outside but from within a noble family. This is one of the hypotheses offered to rescue Abraham, as Chapter 20 somehow tries to do. However, it is certainly a strategy on Abraham's part.

An ambiguous strategy

Third element: what are the consequences? Sarah is taken and brought to Pharaoh's house, Abraham is well-treated, receives flocks, oxen, male and female slaves, donkeys, camels. So, Abraham finds real fortune and is at the height of prosperity. It is Pharaoh who is afflicted with great plagues, even though he had nothing to do with it, all because of Sarah, Abraham's wife. There is a degree of humour here. In the background of this account we seem to see the idea that the Bedouin are smart, while the big landowners are being toyed with and made to pay up.

The conclusion is the discussion, in the final two verses, to resolve the situation, and here we find the moral of the story: 'So Pharaoh called Abraham and said, "What is this you have done to me? Why did you not tell me that she was your wife? Why did you say 'She is my sister?' so that I took her for my wife?"' Here, Pharaoh presents as the honest one: Why did you do this? Because you were afraid? Why were you afraid and why did you give in to your anxieties? Pharaoh sends him off, but with all his gifts.

This same discussion is presented in a more morally decisive way in 20:9. Here, it is Abimelech being spoken of, King of Gerar, who gets up early in the morning after God speaks to him during the night, telling him how things stood. He tells Abraham: 'What have you done to us? How have I sinned against you that you have brought such great guilt on me and my kingdom? You have done things to me that ought not to be done!' There clearly emerges, here, a negative judgement on the ambiguity that Abraham has brought to a wrongful situation, to things that should not be done. This is the structure of the text.

The powerful instinct for self-defence

We now come briefly to the questions: what was Abraham afraid of and what does he do? As is clearly explained in the text, Abraham is afraid they will do him harm because he is a small player, has no kingdom, heads up a small group of shepherds, is beyond protection from any friends, far from his own country, and is defenceless in a hostile world. His anxiety is perfectly understandable. Who could not stand by Abraham's side of the argument? He needs to defend himself from everything and everyone because no one else will think of him. If I don't look after me, who will? I have no relatives, friends, clan who can take revenge on my account.

Abraham is truly afraid that his whole life, the great promise entrusted to him, a great future, could fail, so he must defend himself. This is the immediate instinct of self-defence. What does he do with this fear? He defends himself as best he can, chooses what seems the best strategy at the time. We are certainly impressed by the fact that he could give his wife to someone else!

We need to consider for a moment that Abraham had found no other way. There you have it! Ambiguity has entered the scene. It is not that he did it willingly. He was surely caught in a trap he could not escape from. If he kept his wife he was putting himself at risk, yet if he gave her away there was this ambiguity. He was surrounded, under pressure, and he had found the most convenient way out. Since there was a certain legal pretext, he sought to play with the law, with certain legal possibilities, closing his eyes to the moral aspects because he could do no other.

Yahweh takes pity on poor Abraham

What does Yahweh do? Yahweh does nothing for him, but Yahweh understands him. Abraham is more important, so he is more upset with Pharaoh because (the text does not say so but it is clear) Abraham is in a difficult situation, his fragility emerges. He can do nothing about it and is smothered by it, taken by fear. Yahweh does not rebuke him, does not intervene against him but rebukes the others, even punishing the powerful to make room for and give courage to Abraham. On the one hand, we have Abraham's ambiguous action, while on the other hand, Yahweh's tolerance which will find other means, a new infusion of the kerygma to clarify things, lead him forward.

In this ambiguity of his, Abraham is not silenced by cowardice, lack of faith in the promise, or moral aberration, but is put back in order by patience and peace. God leads him forward by respecting him, watching over, as the Scriptures will then say, closing an eye somewhat to Abraham's fragility and ambiguity. God has other remedies for curing his weakness than loudly rebuking him.

What does this reveal to us about Abraham and Yahweh? Here are the two other questions about Abraham the man, the human being. What does the human being fear? What threatens him? Human beings fear everything that can diminish them, everything that can mortify their lives, possessions, prestige, safety; everything that can place them in embarrassing, unpleasant, confronting situations. There are things we avoid in any way we can, some honest and legitimate, some ambiguous, especially when we find ourselves in difficult situations, ones where there are many hostile forces. When we can sit quietly in our own room we can make plans. But when ambiguous, tense and opposing situations around us are many, when the instinct for self-survival kicks in and we try to get by, we often dabble with ambiguity. Not murder, not dishonesty; I do no harm to anyone, but I try to get by as best I can.

Human reaction, God's reaction

Life's ambiguity, this anxiety, this fear of being diminished, reviled, the fear of loss can refer to many things, not only material goods, and wealth but also to a certain rightful and dutiful prestige; I have to maintain my prestige as a religious, a priest, so I need to prevent one thing or another and employ the means on offer. What do human beings do? They allow themselves to be caught up in anxiety and begin to say, like the dishonest manager in Luke 16: 'What will I do? How to proceed? How can I overcome this situation?' Then they look for expedients in order to resist.

What does God do? It seems to me he does just as he did with Abraham, that is, he has great compassion for these situations of ambiguity and fragility which human beings instinctively fall into. They try not to, might not, do not want to fall, but *ut in pluribus*, as they say, they do fall because of so many outward pressures: the desire not to die, not to lose, not to disappoint others by their own loss is so great that ambiguity arises and becomes part of the fabric of life.

Now, one final question concerning this episode. It is true: Abraham sought to do what he could, felt his way forward, took the first one that came to him, even though he certainly may have felt it was not the best one. But he could not really do otherwise and God did not rebuke him, had compassion on Abraham. However, we can ask ourselves: Can Abraham truly get to know God in this state? Could he arrive at a perfect understanding of God who is revealing himself, giving him complete trust in all these things? Certainly not, because he is being got at by these ambiguities and fears. Hence, even if not morally negative, these fears and ambiguities in reality lead the human being to an unability to fully understand the God who reveals himself only through complete trust in him, total adherence, total abandonment of fears and anxieties. Abraham remains where he is, does not advance, and his understanding of God is blocked. And when this is the case, what happens? What happens is what we see in Chapter 16:1-6.

2. Abraham's fear at home

We move on to a brief consideration of the third episode – Abraham's fear at home, the strategies and expedients he uses. Here, too, we will look at a brief overview of context and structure. We will only take the first six verses of Chapter 16 which tell us how Ishmael was born.

What is the context? Here, too, as in Chapter 12, there is plenty of ambiguity. As soon as he receives one of God's great promises (I will bless you, I will be with you, fear nothing, I will give you this, that...) Abraham adores and thanks God but is overcome by fear. Chapter 16 immediately follows on from the great promise and Covenant of Chapter 15 where God tells Abraham: '"This man (Eliezer of Damascus] shall not be your heir; no one but your very own issue shall be your heir... Look toward heaven and count the stars... so shall your descendants be." And he believed the LORD, and the LORD reckoned it to him as righteousness.'

So, Abraham had made an act of perfect faith, completely abandoned himself to the God of the promise, and this abandonment is marked by an enlightening account: the sacrifice of the animals. Cut in two, a flaming torch passes among them and God's great word is spoken, 'To your descendants I give this land.'

So all the security, the guarantees that Abraham could have, those of a mystical, symbolic nature and those of an experimental nature, he did have. But then comes Chapter 16: 'Now Sarai, Abram's wife, bore him no children. She had an Egyptian slave-girl whose name was Hagar,[2] and Sarai said to Abram, 'You see that the LORD has prevented me from bearing children; go into my slave-girl; it may be that I shall obtain children by her. And Abram listened to the voice of Sarai.' Curious! In Chapter 15, Abraham listened to God's voice and believed, and was reckoned righteous. In Chapter 16, Abram listened to the voice of Sarai. Here is the fragility, the fear of our great father in faith who had received not just the promise of Chapter 12, clearly indicating a son: 'I will make of you a great nation, and I will bless you,' but also the great Covenant of Chapter 15. Yet here once again, he is quickly overcome by fear.

This is the context of the account, Abraham's adventure, as Scripture presents it to us and which I have divided into three parts. The first concerns Sarah's fear: 'You see

---

[2] Up until Chapter 17 of the Book of Genesis, Abraham and Sarah are called Abram and Sarai. But in Chapter 17 God says: 'No longer shall your name be Abram, but your name shall be Abraham; for I have made you the ancestor of a multitude of nations... As for Sarai your wife, you shall not call her Sarai, but Sarah shall be her name' (vv. 5-16).

that the LORD has prevented me from bearing children; go into my slave-girl, it might be that I shall obtain children by her.' The second is Sarah's fear passed on to Abraham: 'Abram listened to the voice of Sarai.' The third is Abraham who, because of Sarah's protests at Hagar's contemptuous behaviour, gives the slave back almost as contemptuously: 'Your slave-girl is in your power; do to her as you please.' Abraham, the man of the promise, is blocked. His understanding of God is eroded, diminished, and he really finds it difficult to live with his situation, his life with the God of the promise.

Our shackles; the root of certain disorders

After having seen Abraham both freed and bound, we can reflect once more on the basis of suggestions offered by St Ignatius in his three colloquies: to consider not our sins but disorder in our life, what is not in order, not fully in line with what should be. The roots of this disorder are our shackles. It is not necessarily a case of serious faults, moral failure, but rather disorder in our choices, our way of living. These are semi-conscious, instinctive shackles it is good to be aware of in the presence of God's word. What would I have done in Abraham's place? When I look at his action, how does that resonate with me? Would I have begun to pray? Would I have fled, faced death, have had the courage to face up to it?

These are some of the resonances Abraham's episode give rise to in us and they allow us to understand what really are the shackles, the ambiguous situations which leave us free when they are dormant but because they are latent, continually risk intruding almost automatically, instinctively, into our way of acting and working.

We should make this examination as contemplation. Just as Abraham did not manage to break the shackles latent in him, and this did not manage to eliminate the ambiguities, do we also not succeed in doing so? And we should be content that God does not rebuke us for our fragility but asks us to recognise it so that with renewed confidence we can submit to the power of his word and ask him: 'Lord, what did you do with Abraham? What do you want to do with us?'

A further two examples of this duplicity

I now offer two New Testament texts which could be useful for exploring the subject matter of this meditation further. The first is Mark 10:17-22, the rich young man, a young man with great desires but very much bound and divided like Abraham. 'Good teacher, what must I do? I want to understand your word deeply,' but then he cannot manage, cannot do so because he cannot escape the routine of daily habits, social position and structure. He listens to the word of God with all good will, throws himself before Jesus in the midst of the people, protests his faith in him, then immediately after says: I can't. The episode repeats Abraham's duplicity.

Another episode that seems to me to have some connection is Luke 19:11-27, the parable of the talents and the ten pounds. Of interest to us is the man who hides his little bit of capital. Why does he do so? Why is he afraid of his master, of himself? Not having gained true knowledge of God, he does not know how to exploit his treasure. He is blocked. Here we see that even certain knowledge of God blocks the person who allows himself to be overcome by fear, then remains blocked behind a kind of servile, religious terror. The word is blocked in him and has not borne fruit. Fear, religious fear of God as conceived of in a certain way, blocks the word in him.

As a prayer for someone who feels bound and wishes to express these shackles before God, I suggest these selected lines from Psalm 31 which can be recited in this context.

> In you, O Lord, I seek refuge,
> in your righteousness deliver me,
> Rescue me speedily,
> Be a rock of refuge for me,
> Into your hand I commend my spirit,
> Be gracious to me, O Lord, for I am in distress;
> My eye wastes away from grief,
> My soul and body also;
> I am the scorn of all my adversaries.

Things are going badly for me. I would be tempted to escape through some personal act of self-defence, whatever it may be 'but in you, O Lord, I seek refuge.'

Fourth Meditation
Gospels for Abraham

It is not without some difficulty that I come this morning to the fundamental texts of Abraham's experience – there are five of them in Genesis 12-15 – to try to understand them with you. The difficulty comes, on the one hand, from the fact that these texts are fundamental for the Christian experience. They are texts the early Christians referred to as a framework for locating Jesus Christ within the history of salvation and to take account of who he was for them and for the world. On the other hand, these texts are so distant from us, so in approaching them there is the risk of almost being disappointed.

What do these texts speak of? Can they be compared to the gospel? Let us try to meditate on them, bearing in mind not only the difficulty but, in my view, the value of considering them in reference, for example, to Acts 2:39 where Peter says, at the end of his address: 'For the promise is for you, for your children, and for all who are far away, everyone whom the Lord God calls to him.' So, the promise made to Abraham is also for those far away, for us who were far away, called by the Lord our God. There is a direct link between the promise to Abraham and what the New Testament experienced. Furthermore, in the *Benedictus* it says that the Lord 'remembered the oath,' which has come true, 'that he swore to our ancestor Abraham.' In this spirit we would like to reflect on some of the Genesis texts that speak of Abraham and which some other passages from Paul also refer to.

What are these gospels?

The title I have given this meditation, 'gospels for Abraham', could sound a bit odd. And really, the first title I thought of giving it was 'The kerygma for Abraham', that is, what is the proclamation of salvation Abraham receives which God gives him? But then I saw that there were various proclamations and, which is also significant, other later ones, so we would need to speak of kerygmas. But since this word doesn't sound right in the plural, I put it into New Testament terms: gospels for Abraham, or in other words, proclamations of salvation given Abraham. This plural word can also help us better understand the New Testament texts themselves. However, in more direct Old Testament words, one could say 'promises for Abraham', or 'oaths for Abraham'. They are all ways of expressing God's activity, his kerygmatic, evangelising, consoling, comforting and clarifying activity for Abraham.

Here we are entering into the dynamic of the *Exercises*, Second Week: Jesus who proclaims, as the prelude to the meditation on the Kingdom says, 'Jesus went about proclaiming through cities and villages.' We will place ourselves directly before the 'gospels for Abraham', the proclamations of salvation given to Abraham which help us understand the proclamations of salvation which Jesus gives us.

This is the dynamic process of the meditation, which I shall offer in four points. The first point: the texts and how they are structured. Second point: three questions we will put to Abraham, bearing in mind these texts. Third point: a question to ourselves, what similarities and differences are there between these 'gospels' and the New Testament Gospel? And finally, the fourth point: what are the similarities and differences and the connections between these proclamations and what is given us in the meditation on the Kingdom.

1. Salvation texts

Let's look at the texts first of all, beginning with the fundamental one, Genesis 12:1-4:

> Now the LORD said to Abram, 'Go from your country and your kindred and your father's house to the land that I will show you. I will make of you a great nation, and I will bless you, and make your name great, so that you will be a blessing. I will bless those who bless you, and the one who curses you I will curse; and in you all the families of the earth shall be blessed.'
> So Abram went as the LORD had told him; and Lot went with him.

This first text has an introduction and three elements. The introduction is, 'The LORD said to Abram.' As commentators note, here we are beginning from zero, so to speak, as is recorded in the first chapter of Genesis: 'God said let there be light.' We are witnessing a primordial divine initiative. The sentence 'The LORD said to Abram' is the principle and foundation of the whole story of Abraham; he did not seek God out, but God sought out Abraham. We could compare it to the 'Principle and Foundation' of the *Exercises*: man was created to know and serve God just as Abraham, thanks to God's initiative, was called by God to be his own. This initiative is expressed in that single word 'said'. This is God's word entering into dialogue with Abraham, and with him it creates the history of salvation.

What does this word of God consist of? First of all – the first element – it holds an imperative, 'Go, leave'. Here we can note how all-embracing this is; country, kindred, father's home, everything that makes up the setting of Abraham's life, not just the restricted family setting but everything that could sustain him in the social setting: clan, mentality, culture etc. He leaves all these things and goes 'to the land that I will show you.' This land is not identified, it is indicated generally. What and where are not said and are part of the mystery of God. It is God's word which will indicate these things and this word demands total abandonment.

Promises made to Abraham

Second element: the many promises are all in the future and follow on from the imperative in the present: 'Go', 'I will make of you a great nation, I will bless you, I will make your name great, you will be a blessing, I will bless those who bless you and the one who curses you I will curse; and in you all the families of the earth shall be blessed.' Here we have six verbs or verb phrases indicating future divine activity with Abraham, and which are the kerygma.

I note here that we often insist on the words 'go', 'leave', 'depart'. This is not the kerygma. But only a condition. The kerygma, the proclamation for Abraham is: 'I will bless you' etc. The kerygma for Abraham is the fullness of blessing – the word 'blessing' is repeated five times in various forms – and will be a universal completeness somehow touching all humankind. For Abraham it is something grand, amazing. Clearly, it is good to stress Abraham's faith in the unknown, but it is very important to highlight the fact that this faith is sustained by a word of consolation, promise, future potential capable of completely filling Abraham's heart and which will be the secret of his entire life. The kerygma is not so much the order to go in itself, but the order linked with a fullness of promises and prospects not in the singular but all-embracing, a great nation outlined, a new humanity.

The words 'In you all the families of the earth shall be blessed' could seem a bit obscure. Some would give it a simpler interpretation, meaning that families of the earth would bless one another one day but by saying to one another: blessed are you like Abraham. That would be one form of blessing and Abraham would be happy that they say it. However, already in the Old Testament, the Book of Sirach (Ecclesiasticus) and the Septuagint, then the New

Testament, interpreted them in a much stronger, more eloquent sense: in you all will be blessed, that is, you will be the cause of blessing for all. This is how Paul interprets it in the Letter to the Galatians and elsewhere. So there is the perspective of a great people, a unity of human beings in Abraham. Here is the message, the kerygma, the gospel for Abraham.

Third element of the scene: 'So Abram went.' He went with all those closest to him, a detail which will help us understand something of the New Testament. 'Abram took his wife Sarai, and his brother's son Lot, and all the possessions that they had gathered, and the persons they had acquired in Haran; and they set forth to go to the land of Canaan.' Abraham did not leave poor, but with all he had and his retinue. But he does depart with an act of total trust and, as the Letter to the Hebrews says, not knowing where he was going but trusting totally in God's word.

Land and descendants

This is the first proclamation. The second is in v. 7: Abraham arrives in the land of Canaan as far as Shechem, near the Oak of Moreh. 'At the time, the Canaanites were in the land. Then the LORD appeared to Abram, and said, "To your offspring I will give this land."'

Here it specifies 'this land'. But also note the contrast: the Canaanites lived in this land, meaning they owned it through arms, power, the fullness of powers, yet the Lord tells Abraham, who has entered as a migrant without power, that he will give it to him and his descendants. Here is a new kerygma for Abraham, a new proclamation which picks up the first and makes it specific.

Furthermore, after Abraham made the great gesture of generosity by leaving to Lot the part that would become the worst but at the time was the better portion, the Lord again tells Abraham in 13:14-18; '"Raise your eyes now, and look from the place where you are, northward and southward and eastward and westward [this is a 360° perspective]; for all the land that you see I will give to your offspring forever. I will make your offspring like the dust of the earth; so if one can count the dust of the earth, your offspring also can be counted. Rise up, walk through the length an breadth of the land, for I will give it to you." So Abram moved his tent, and came and settled by the oaks of Mamre, which are at Hebron, and there he built an altar to the LORD.'

Here, we find only two of the three earlier elements; there is no more 'go' but there is the kerygma: look at this land; it is all yours and your descendants'. The by now two key terms are specified: land and descendants. Abraham needs both, since it is of little value to have the descendants if he does not have the land, nor does it help to have the land if there are no descendants. This breadth of descendants and land specifies the promise which is extended pretty much without limits, descendants 'like the dust of the earth.' But it is a promise for the future and it is moving to see how Abraham accepts in faith the invitation to walk the length and breadth of the land that is not his, to make himself aware of what the Lord will give him.

Abraham makes this act of trust in God's word: 'Rise up, walk through the length and breadth of the land for I will give it to you' (13:17) could be compared with the first element of 12:1-5: 'Go'. This future 'I will give' does seem a bit ridiculous, nevertheless. Why isn't it in the present as 'I am now giving you…'? But no, it is 'I will give it to you, and in the meantime walk through it, get to know it, savour it in faith, confidence, hope. It is not yet yours, but go and find out about this land. Abraham moved his tents and went to settle 'by the oaks of Mamre, which are at Hebron; and there he built an altar to the LORD.' Carrying out this command shows Abraham's faith, building altars here and there, stones, to say: the Lord is here. First at Shechem, then Mamre, almost as a way of taking possession at least notionally, figuratively, of this land which is already his, he takes possession in faith.

We finally come to Chapter 15, usually presented as a single chapter but I want to split it in two (1-6; 7-18) because to me it seems to be two episodes brought together but which can be structured separately.

Abraham believed in God

'After these things,' after the victory over the four kings, and Melchisedek's sacrifice, 'the word of the LORD came to Abram in a vision: "do not be afraid, Abram, I am your shield, your reward shall be very great."'

Here the kerygma changes somewhat. It is consoling: do not fear, have faith, I am your shield. It is a more personalised kerygma, it does not talk about land. It is God who will do something for Abraham, so have faith, the reward will be great. 'But Abram said, "O Lord GOD, what will you give me, for I continue childless, and the heir of my house is Eliezer of Damascus?" And Abram said, "You have given me no offspring, and so a slave born in my house is to be my heir." But the word of the LORD came to him, "This man shall not be your heir; no one but your very own issue shall be your heir." He brought him outside and said, "Look toward heaven and count the stars, if you are able to count them." Then he said to him, "So shall your descendants be." And he believed the LORD; and the LORD reckoned it to him as righteousness.'

Note the last verse, v. 6, fundamental to the whole of Pauline theology.

Here is the structure of the text. God's consolation: do not fear I will be with you; Abraham's lament: but what ever is that if I have no heir? God's renewed assurance: look at the heavens, the countless stars, if you are able to count them; and finally the execution, which is not of something material or symbolic like the first one where he left with all his possessions, walked through the land, built altars. Here, Abraham 'believed.' Of all of Abraham's ways of carrying things out, Paul chose this last as the typical Abrahamic way of doing so; he believed, entrusted himself and was reckoned as righteous.

The Covenant sacrifice

The final text, which follows on immediately, is Chapter 15:7 ff., the Covenant sacrifice. Here, the promise, the kerygma, is given in another form and in another context, one of sacrifice.

> Then he said to him, 'I am the LORD who brought you from Ur of the Chaldeans, to give you this land to possess.' But he said, 'O Lord GOD, how am I to know that I shall posses it?' He said to him, 'Bring me a heifer three years old, a ram three years old, a turtledove and a young pigeon.' He bought him all this and cut them in two, laying each half over against the other; but he did not cut the birds in two. And when birds of prey came down on the carcasses, Abram drove them away. As the sun was going down, a deep sleep fell upon Abram and a deep and terrifying darkness descended upon him. Then the LORD said to Abram, 'know this for certain, that your offspring shall be aliens in a land that is not theirs, and shall be slaves there, and they shall be oppressed for four hundred years; but I will bring judgement on the nation that they serve, and afterwards they shall come out with great possessions. As for yourself, you shall go to your ancestors in peace; you shall be buried in a good old age. And they shall come back here in the fourth generation; for the iniquity of the Amorites is not yet complete.' When the sun had gone down and it was dark, a smoking fire pot and a flaming torch passed between these pieces. On that day, the LORD

made a Covenant with Abram, saying, 'To your descendants I give this land, from the river of Egypt to the great river, the river Euphrates…'

The structure here is complex and other elements are involved. It begins with a self-presentation: 'I am the LORD who brought you from Ur of the Chaldeans.' God reminds him of the first intervention, his first initiative with Abraham. But Abraham's reply is querulous: how will I know? Abraham makes problems, is wavering, finds it an effort to accept the kerygma. It is not like the first time when he obeys immediately. Then follows the scene of the sacrifice with the dream revelation. It is a scene replete with mysterious symbolism. Some say the birds of prey represent the misfortune to come, the descent into Egypt. At any rate, we are in a situation of fear and fright which is then clarified by the revelation in the dream that is not really good news: you will die, they will go to Egypt, but I will take care of your people.

Here, from something general, the kerygma becomes more specific: I will look after you in some concrete circumstances of your life, so don't be frightened if some things don't immediately go as you imagined. God continuously adapts the proclamation, makes it clear for individual situations, specifies it according to different times in Abraham's life. Unfortunately, the revelation in the dream is not altogether pleasant: there is a long wait ahead, but I will be with your people. Finally, the last moment of this kerygma, the torch, the fire pot passing through, signifies the Covenant and the promise: 'To your descendants I give this land.' The two elements are there again: descendants and land. Here then, briefly presented, are the five kerygmatic steps telling us what God said to Abraham.

What do these texts teach us?

Summing up, we can make some general observations. First of all, as we were saying, we are amazed at the number of kerygmas or gospels for Abraham, the many promises, not just one, one different from the other. But there is a common basis, descendants and land, with some applications according to specific moments in Abraham's life. What does this mean? That a simple word of God is not enough for Abraham. Of itself, God's word spoken directly to Abraham should contain everything and be enough for his entire life. Why did God reveal himself in stages? Because there was a need for Abraham that he repeat, clarify, apply, specify; the kerygma for Abraham is fundamentally one, but diversified in its application to individual circumstances of his life.

These proclamations or gospels, or promises, differ among themselves not only in their content but also in their formal structure. The imperative predominates in some: go; the future in others: I will give you a nation, a land. The execution that follows is sometimes prompt, sometimes querulous, and problems arise; sometimes there are other aspects like the Covenant sacrifice, the dream at night. So God reveals himself to Abraham in a variety of words and circumstances. Nevertheless, it seems clear from all these modes of expression – as is evident in 12:1 – that we are dealing with free, creative acts of God. God is freely advancing his plan, his initiative of salvation. God is doing something new on earth. This novelty is a great people, descendants. It is not simply a personal, consoling initiative in Abraham's life but the reality of a great nation which reappears in different ways as an outline on the horizon in the fullness of divine blessings.

2. Three questions to put to Abraham

The second point: keeping in mind the texts we have meditated on, I suggest putting three questions to Abraham. The first could be expressed thus: what situation did you find yourself in, Abraham, when the word of God came to you? The second: what were you waiting for? The third: what did the kerygma give you?

To the first question, Abraham would reply: I was going pretty well, was fairly wealthy. Perhaps I had achieved a degree of religious balance, but I was a nomad, had no land, so I was not like others who were landowners, who could count on a safe place to settle in. In Genesis 11:27 it says that Abraham was a descendant of them, son of Ferah, brother of Nahor and Haran. 'Abram and Nahor took wives; the name of Abram's wife was Sarai, and the name of Nahor's wife was Milcah. She was the daughter of Haran the father of Milcah and Iscah. Now Sarai was barren; she had no child.' (29 ff.)

Before Abraham comes on the scene as the beneficiary of God's word, he was already pointed to as the man without children. From a social perspective he was not only a nomad without his own land, but also without a future. So what was Abraham waiting for? Abraham could say: I was waiting for what a man of that time without land and children would be waiting for, since it was such a sad fate to end up as a nobody in practical terms. My wealth would go to others, others would pass them on but I, Abraham, will have no future. My life has no future. So this is what Abraham could reasonably expect.

What would he say about the kerygma? The kerygma tells him quite the opposite to this, about a land and a people; a land he does not have and a people he has no right to, and all this in unlimited fashion like the stars in the heavens, the land on the seashore. Here is the kerygma for Abraham, the promise that fills his life and, because accepted in faith, it allows him to leave, journey, wander, even though not having what he expects at the time. His heart is filled with the great word of God. It filled his life and is the principle, the point of reference for all other chances he takes. It is the single point that allows us to describe why Abraham acts, does what he does, why he is capable of these things. It is because he has already received, in faith, a share in the fullness of God.

3. The 'gospels' in the Old Testament, and the New Testament Gospel

We now come to the third point. If this is the kerygma for Abraham, what are the similarities and differences between kerygmas and the New Testament Gospel, i.e. with what Jesus proclaims in the New Testament? I believe we can more concretely understand the Gospel proclamation for ourselves if we make reference to this first, typological, exemplary divine initiative of the proclamation, promises and 'gospels' given to Abraham.

To start us off on this point, I am offering some New Testament Gospel examples pulled together from here and there, Gospels or proclamations with similarities, including formal ones, to Abraham's kerygma and which reproduce the three elements: imperative, future promise, execution of the command.

A typical case of formal similarity is Mark 1:17-18: '"Follow me and I will make you fish for people." And immediately they left their nets and followed him.' Note here the identical structure to Genesis 12:15: the imperative 'follow me' – leave your land, the future. 'I will make you fish for people' – I will give you a land, I will make you a great nation. Here is the promise: you will be fishermen and have a future. This is your future, more or less simple, more or less reassuring but not too exultant. Yet, I will change it totally and will have you fishing for a great nation: 'And immediately they followed him,' leaving their nets. There is an interesting difference of response here to the kerygma. While in Abraham's case it says he left taking everything he had with him, here it says 'they left their nets and followed him,' stressing the fact that following Jesus calls for more total detachment still than for Abraham. This kerygma refers to a particular situation, one of apostolate or discipleship.

In another kerygma, Mark 1:15: 'The time is fulfilled and the kingdom of God has come near, repent and believe in the good news,' we have two of the three elements: the kerygmatic or 'good news' element; 'The time is fulfilled, the kingdom of God is near,' the wait is over. Then comes the condition, the imperative: 'repent and believe.' There are many examples of the kerygma in the Gospel and it would be interesting to find and list them.

Luke and Matthew give us three texts

A Gospel kerygma which closely resembles Genesis 15:1-6, where a word of consolation is prevalent, is in Luke 12:32-33, which seems to echo Abraham's querulous response: but I have no descendants. And he is told: 'Do not be afraid, Abram, I am your shield.' When the disciples say: we have followed you but we are few in number, are doing little and the people don't follow, then comes the consoling word: 'Do not be afraid, little flock, for it is your Father's good pleasure to give you the kingdom.' The kingdom is yours, rest assured, the Father gives it to you. Then the imperative: sell your possessions and give alms. Make purses for yourselves that do not wear out, an unfailing treasure in heaven where no thief comes near and no moth destroys.

Here we have consolation, the proclamation of the

kerygma, and the condition which always relates to the kerygma. Jesus does not ask for an heroic act without reason. Faced with the 'sell your possessions' there is the promise of the kingdom. Another example of kerygma where the consolatory aspect prevails is Matthew 11:28-29: 'Come to me all you who are weary and are carrying heavy burdens and I will give you rest. Take my yoke upon you, and learn from me; for I am gentle and humble in heart, and you will find rest for your souls. For my yoke is easy and my burden is light.' The 'learn from me' is imperative, and the 'you will find rest' is consoling. I will give you fullness of rest, life, the experience you are seeking.

Another form of kerygma is in Luke 10:21-22, even though in typical New Testament form.

> At the same hour Jesus rejoiced in the
> Holy Spirit and said, 'I thank you, Father,
> Lord of heaven and earth, because you
> have hidden these things from the wise
> and the intelligent and have revealed them
> to infants; yes Father, for such was your
> gracious will. All things have been handed
> over to me by my Father, and no one knows
> who the son is except the Father, or who
> the Father is except the Son and anyone
> to whom the Son chooses to reveal him.'

Here, the central proclamation is: the Father will be known through the Son. It is a proclamation of salvation, a certain way of presenting the announcement, the gospel.

Proclamations in Paul and Revelations

To also mention some examples of proclamation in Paul, one typical expression among others is Galatians 2:20: 'and it is no longer I who live, but it is Christ who lives in me. And the life I now live in the flesh I live by faith in the Son of God, who loved me and gave himself for me.' It is the proclamation of what Paul feels and is living at that moment as the fullness of the promise for him: Christ lives in me.

A proclamation for the faithful is Colossians 1:27: 'To them God chose to make known how great among the Gentiles are the riches of the glory of this mystery, which is Christ in you, the hope of glory.' It is the fullness of the kerygma, the proclamation which clearly has dimensions which are sometimes pastoral, at times about apostolic commitment, and sometimes concerns cosmic dimensions at the level of the fullness of the people of God.

Again, we can mention Revelations 21:1-5, which is among the best examples of New Testament kerygma, a proclamation in historical form and concerning the people of God.

> Then I saw a new heaven and a new earth; for the first heaven and the first earth had passed away, and the sea was no more. And I saw the holy city, the new Jerusalem, coming down out of Heaven from God, prepared as a bride adorned for her husband. And I heard a loud voice from the throne saying, 'See, the home of God is among mortals. He will dwell with them; they will

be his peoples, and God himself will be with them; he will wipe every tear from their eyes. Death will be no more; mourning and crying and pain will be no more, for the first things have passed away.' And the one who was seated on the throne said, 'See, I am making all things new.'

This is the central element of the kerygma for Abraham, referred to New Testament fullness: in you all nations of the earth will be blessed, the fullness of blessing for the new humanity.

4. The Old Testament Kingdom and the New Testament Kingdom

After looking at some of these New Testament Gospels, we can draw out some considerations of a general nature.

1. The substantial subject of Jesus' kerygma is 'the Kingdom': the Kingdom of God is near. But it is specified in different ways according to differing situations: at one moment it emphasises consolation in response to a doubt, a problem; at another, it looks to the future, the fullness of the heavenly Jerusalem; at another moment it emphasises a task entrusted to people in the kingdom. But all this wealth of approaches and variety can substantially be reduced to the kingdom.

2. The idea of detachment appears to be more pronounced than in the Abrahamic kerygma. Leaving their nets they followed him; go, sell your possessions and give them to the poor. It is telling us that the New Testament kerygma will be

richer, more complete and total for human beings because of the detachment it proposes and demands.

3. The New Testament kerygma's insistence is sometimes on the present where faith needs to be exercised; we need to live in faith. Sometimes it is on the future, and then hope prevails.

4. It all relates to Jesus: Jesus present, Jesus who calls, Jesus who is followed. Even if he is not always clearly named, it is clear that at the heart of everything is the person of Jesus, the richness he represents for us, for the people who are in Jesus, the fullness of the heavenly Jerusalem which lives and is built around the Lamb.

So far I have not mentioned the fundamental expression of the New Testament kerygma, the unique one to which all the others are reduced and which is interesting to bring into alignment with the others, otherwise it is too rich, and its textuality may not be specified. It is this: He who died lives, Christ who died, is risen. This is the heart of the kerygma but it can be specified in very many of its aspects.

It is important to understand the richness of this central formula, so it does not remain just words. Because it preserves the richness which truly corresponds to the fullness of the kingdom, we need to link this central formula to many others as God did with Abraham, presenting it in many ways according to need, but all clearly referring to its core, which for Abraham was land and people. In the New Testament it is Jesus, Son of God made man and risen for us. It is the promise of a kingdom, a people.

Relationships between these proclamations and the Ignatian 'kingdom'

Let us conclude this last point by looking at the meditation on the kingdom. According to St Ignatius, the emphasis in this meditation falls on commitment. Christ, the 'eternal king', says: whoever wishes to follow me must do as I do. However, this should not cause us to lose sight of the true balance between things, because it is not the kerygma *per se*: do as I do, or leave everything, work by day, be vigilant by night. The kerygma is: 'it is my will to conquer the whole world,' that is, the fullness of the kingdom Jesus offers his followers, the fullness of the kingdom of God, the New Jerusalem, Christ as richness for everyone who follows him; and by virtue of this fullness received, the demand emerges: follow me where I am, the conditions being a humble, poor life embraced in view of this fullness.

My final suggestion for today: after having looked at some New Testament texts we could meditate on, the questions each one could pose for himself are as follows: How does the kerygma for Abraham and for the early Christians present itself to me? Which of these New Testament aspects is clear and comprehensible to me, or which, like for Abraham, do I come into conflict with? We need to admit that, like Abraham, some conflict with the kerygma can arise. Hence, we need to enter into dialogue with the kerygma too, just as it shows itself to us in both its light and shade.

As a prayer text, among other possibilities I suggest the *Benedictus*, which is praise for what God is doing according to the promise made to Abraham. However, by examining the *Benedictus*, the circumstance in which it was said and the situation it refers to – the birth of John the Baptist and his destiny which will be to die from decapitation – we clearly see how this kerygma is coloured in a particular way by following Christ. But it is still a moment for realisation of the promises made to Abraham, including in difficult situations such as those in John the Baptist's life, where this promise is manifested in a rather disconcerting way. Yet, to the eyes of faith, this promise made to Abraham already exists as real, true anticipation. The fullness God gives in serving him without fear in holiness and righteousness. This, too, is one of the aspects of God's promises we can reflect and meditate on.

Fifth Meditation
Abraham's social behaviour: Abraham and social justice

The subject of today's meditation involves some smaller episodes in Abraham's life which are theologically significant and are often left aside as just little stories based on legends. But seen in the context of the promise (everything about the historical Abraham revolves around this promise from God, just as we, within the context of Abraham as a type, are enlightened and enriched by this promise), it seems to me that these small episodes, which are somewhat marginal, take on meaning and let us see how Abraham behaves in different circumstances of life, once enlightened by the kerygma. Perhaps we could give our meditation this title: 'Abraham's social behaviour: Abraham and social justice.' In other words, how the kerygma leads Abraham to regulate his behaviour towards others, things, situations, others' rights.

Groans of prayer, groans of creation

In this regard, I recall a very important reflection we can draw from an article by Cullmann in which he speaks of groans of prayer. In what was novel for me, even though exegetes have always noted it, he relates these groans to the ones St Paul speaks of in Romans 8:22: 'We know that the whole of creation has been groaning in labour pains until now.' All the suffering and groans of creation, not just the immaterial part, but all of creation which suffers due to unjust, erroneous behaviour which we do not understand; all the groans of the human world living without apparent meaning and yearning for a meaningful life, life with purpose, a minimum of significance. All these groans Cullmann connects with Romans 8:23: 'but we ourselves… Groan inwardly while we wait for adoption.'

We give voice and clarity to these groans of creation which we are part of, we too groan because of the lack of meaning in situations we endure, and we give these groans expression in prayer. And in these expressions it is the 'Spirit who intercedes with sighs too deep for words' (8:26), making them his, taking on the groans of the world, our groans, in perfect adoration of the Father. It is when we achieve this level of clarity that we are urged on to perfect justice and to work for justice.

I believe this is the only motive which enables us to detach ourselves from everything and spend time quietly for some days in prayer. It is not, as it might sometimes seem, a luxury or something strange. There is need for so many things in the world, there are so many people suffering, and what do I do? In reality, in prolonged, arduous, profound prayer entrusted to the Spirit, we unite ourselves mysteriously but really with the groans of all our brothers and sisters – this teaching we can draw from Paul – sharing inwardly with them, and freeing up our heart to serve them in justice.

This is what gives rise to the true service of others, which is not simply the expression of immediate compassion or a rush of enthusiasm which then dissipates, as often happens. It is service matured in sighs too deep for words, which come from contemplation of the meaninglessness of the human situation and from opening up to others. God's power sustains this through his gospel. We aspire to it. We would like to bring to this service all those who in some way share in this inner groaning of our prayer. Through it, we share in the tremendous suffering of so many of our brothers and sisters, particularly those in search of a meaning to give their lives, and to the world we live in. I say this to introduce us to these very simple little episodes in which the behaviours that I said we could call Abraham's social behaviour, his 'social justice', nevertheless become apparent.

These episodes are linked with others we have already read in Genesis 12: Abraham's call, and Abraham in Egypt.

It is interesting to note the nobility, the greatness of Abraham's call, then Abraham's ambiguity in Egypt. This is followed in Chapter 13, which we will read, by the episode of Abraham's generosity. Hence Abraham's life proceeds a little like ours with moments of light, moments of weakness, then new moments of recovery, and so it slowly matures until it reaches the fullness of understanding of God.

1. Abraham divides the land with Lot

What does the first episode, Genesis 13:1-18, say? The situation is described in the first six verses. Abraham and Lot are wealthy, very much and even too much so; too much because at a certain point their over-abundant flocks could not go on together. Each mostly looked after his own flock, asking local inhabitants for permission once the harvest was over. Up to a certain limit this is possible, after which they find they need to split, otherwise there would be problems. Abraham and Lot had become enormously wealthy and, as always happens with wealth, problems begin to emerge. While they were poor or had less stuff, they helped one another and were in agreement. Now, reasons for dispute were emerging.

This is the first part of the episode. It would be interesting to go into detail to highlight some of the niceties of the text. But sticking to the essentials, we see that a quarrel arises, not between Abraham and Lot (the text puts it very delicately) but between Abraham's and Lot's herders. As often happens, the great personalities let others do the fighting, do not intervene, and keep their dignity intact. But it is clear that at a certain point the two had to sort things out. The quarrel arises, so the text tells us at v. 7, while 'the Canaanites and Perizzites lived in the land': so they are still in a difficult situation, still guests, strangers at risk. Any quarrel between them is certainly harmful, inauspicious, and could destroy their wealth.

A generous offer

Second part: Abraham's offer in vv. 8-9, Abraham tells Lot: 'Let there be no strife between you and me, and between your herders and my herders; for we are kindred. Is not the whole land before you? Separate yourself from me. If you take the left hand, then I will go to the right; or if you take the right hand, then I will go to the left.' Here, then, is Abraham's offer, a hugely generous one, quite exceptional.

Finally, Lot's choice, extensively described. As von Rad notes well in his commentary, Lot's inner decision-making process is described visually: 'Lot looked about him and saw that the plain of the Jordan was well-watered everywhere like the garden of the LORD.' He had already seen it earlier but here it is emphasised to show how Lot comes to his decision and his reasons for it. Looking from Bethel, down toward the east, he sees that the place 'before the LORD had destroyed Sodom and Gomorrah,' was like the Lord's garden, like the land of Egypt in the direction of Zoar. 'So Lot chose for himself all the plain of the Jordan and Lot journeyed eastward' (vv. 10-11).

After Lot's choice comes the execution: 'thus they separated from each other. Abram settled in the land of Canaan [to the left, to the west] and Lot settled among the cities of the Plain and moved his tent as far as Sodom. Now the people of Sodom were wicked, great sinners against the LORD.' This is a small bit of information that prepares for what will happen in Chapter 19, but we can already guess. Lot thinks he has chosen the better part and has no idea what he has got himself into, or the problems his greed will lead to. So on the one hand, we have Lot's choice and on the other, Abraham's calm acceptance.

We have already meditated on the last part of the episode, the second promise: 'the LORD said to Abram, after Lot had separated from him, "Raise your eyes now and look from the place where you are, northward and southward and eastward and westward."' At the 'raise your eyes,' Abraham could have been a bit disappointed. Lot has gone to the better spot. What will I do? 'for all the land that you see I will give to you and to your offspring forever. I will make your offspring like the dust of the earth...' This is the conclusion to the episode.

Here, then, are the stages of the text: Abraham and Lot are too wealthy; there is fighting among the herders, then come Abraham's conciliatory offer, Lot's acceptance and choice of the better part, Abraham's quiet acceptance of what remains, but God gives Abraham another promise in a grand vision, much greater that the previous one, of all the land to the four points of the compass.

Now, let us meditate on this passage and its points, including psychological ones; how the human soul behaves, how it behaves in conflict situations. I suggest these very simple reflections.

Abraham's generosity

First: Abraham could have demanded much from Lot. Lot was a small orphan when Abraham had adopted him, raised him with love, looked after him, had perhaps taught him the art of sheep-farming, so if he had become wealthy he probably owed it to Abraham's interest and protection. Abraham could expect subjection, humility, submission, acceptance from Lot. Instead, he not only treats him as an equal, which we are already struck by, but as a brother: not a nephew he was doing something for, for free, and who should yield to him. Lot owed him everything and he should not be disturbing his pastures. Had Abraham insisted on his rights, Lot would not have been involved with his pastures, but Abraham treats him like a brother who he does not need to quarrel with. It is better to seek agreement. In fact, and this is unprecedented, he treats him as if he were his first-born son. Abraham could have said: we are looking to divide the land as brothers in an equitable, just way, bearing in mind that you have already received so much from me and that all the things you have, you owe to me. So now be happy with this. This would have been a just approach among brothers. Instead, Abraham gave him first-born rights, almost head of family rights: 'Go where you want to, is not the whole land in front of you? I will choose what you don't want.'

This is the height of generosity, given that we are dealing with a greedy man, or at least one content with possessions acquired by the work of his own hands. This exceptional largesse, Abraham's humility and detachment, are a surprise to us. But what surprises us more is that Abraham accepts Lot's choice and sets himself up in the land of Canaan. When we make generous offerings like this, it is always so the other may still have a problem or two, or in other words we think the other person will understand that he has to choose what is his due and nothing more. We can be quite irritated when the other does not understand this and takes what is ours. In fact, by letting the other make the decision, it is really so that person can be reduced to his appropriate limits. But Abraham is faultless here and freely accepts what Lot has rejected, and does so very calmly. This is surprising. He was not just pretending, was not practising the shrewd art of having the best while appearing to be generous. It was a sincere expression of the simplicity of his heart, something quite rare among human beings.

Abraham's wealth; the kerygma

Now the second reflection. What is it that gives Abraham this completely Ignatian indifference, complete availability, freedom of heart and generosity to say: 'you be the first to choose and I will be happy with what you did not choose?' The text does not tell us. It doesn't go to such psychological lengths. But if we read it within the context of the promise, it seems to me that we are led to say that Abraham has something more within, a treasure in his heart. It is right that Lot take the greater wealth – Abraham has the promise. This promise is a greater treasure to him than anything else and it makes him free, calm, available and ready to give the other the best.

And that is how it was, even if the text does not say so. I am drawing this from the context where everything is to be interpreted in view of the promise. But the text does give us a bit of a grip on this, as some exegetes point out. If we compare Abraham's words to Lot (v. 9): 'Is not the whole land before you?' with God's words to Abraham: 'Raise your eyes now, and look from the place where you are... for all the land that you see I will give you' (v. 14 ff.) then we see a very special correspondence. If Abraham was able to tell Lot: here is the whole land, you choose! It is because God had told Abraham: Here it all is. I am giving it to you. Not just a portion of land but all of it from east to west, north to south and I will make your descendants like the dust of the earth. It seems to me that here is a correspondence between Abraham's generosity and God's promise, a promise which is now a constant presence in his life. Abraham has this great wealth which is the kerygma and it sets him free, at peace, makes him calm, available, ready.

Abraham and the four great kings

Now let us look at the second episode, Chapter 14, which follows on immediately, especially verses 1-16; the four kings versus the five kings and Abraham. One commentator says that this chapter is a world unto itself, a chapter that belongs to none of the Yahwist, Elohist or Priestly sources. We do not know where it comes from. It contains a mixture of ancient data oddly mixed between them and with apparent exaggeration. It has bewildered all the exegetes, especially in the first half. The second half, where it speaks of Melchizedek, has been much exploited but we won't deal with it just yet.

The first part seems to involve ancient legends, stories of great battles between kings, and at a certain point a story about Abraham is inserted. The Jerusalem Bible says of this chapter: 'There are different judgements as to its value. It seems it is a late composition but it remains an ancient one... It is historically impossible that Elam would ever have dominated the cities south of the Dead Sea.' But let us try to draw some theological value from the chapter, though it seems to hold little of that. I will divide it into four sections.

Lot is saved – along with his possessions

– The first part describes the war between the four great kings from the north, the greatest names that could be chosen: King Amraphel of Shinar, King Arioch of Ellasar, King Chedorlaomer of Elam, and King Tidal of Goiim (that is, the king of the peoples). Indicated here are Babylonia, the Elamites, hence the great northern kingdoms with some strange names, some corresponding to likely ones. The idea is that the great Northern Empires are heading south against the small tribes in Palestine where there are little kingdoms. They cause a massacre. This is described in vv. 1-3.

– The second part, vv. 4-7, tells how the small Palestinian tribes were subjected to Chedorlaomer, the Elamite king, for 12 years but rebelled in the thirteenth year. In the fourteenth year, these four kings became allies and defeated the Rephaim at Ashteroth-Karnaim, the Zuzim etc. as far as El-Paran, which borders on the desert. Then they came to En-Mispat, Kadesh, and devastated all the territory of the

Amalekites and the Amorites. Thus, all the most warlike and strongest tribes were wiped out.

– As we can see, the picture is grandiose, truculent and deliberately exaggerated. But this is not enough – here is the third point, vv. 9-12 – because the little kings from the territory of Sodom and Gomorrah try to resist, but they are also defeated and Lot is captured during it. After having chosen the best part, he now immediately finds himself in trouble because, as the text says, 'they also took Lot, the son of Abraham's brother, who lived in Sodom, and his goods, and departed.'

– The fourth part, vv. 13-16, simply says that 'one who had escaped, came and told Abraham the Hebrew, who was living by the oaks of Mamre the Amorite' (hence further south)… 'When Abram heard that his nephew had been taken captive, he led forth his trained men born in his house, three hundred eighteen of them, and went in pursuit as far as Dan. He divided his forces against them by night, he and his servants, and routed them and pursued them to Hobah, north of Damascus.' Hence, they pursued them for hundreds of kilometres. 'Then he brought back all the goods, and also brought back his nephew Lot with his goods, and the women and the people.' Here, we clearly have a grandiose, deliberately exaggerated description, but this also forces us to reflect.

The reflections I propose are as follows:

Three reflections

The first reflection is that Abraham does not seem to reason things through; he is facing a disproportionate risk, 318 men against the four northern kings. The disproportion is such as to make us think of a deeply theological significance without which, historically, we do not see what significance to give it. The four great kings had defeated much more powerful tribes: Amalekites, Amorites. They had devastated all the centre of Palestine, so we could conclude – following what is said when contemplating the Kingdom, Christ's plan as 'eternal king' – that Abraham here has neither judgement nor reason. Ignatius had said: 'Consider that all those who have judgement and reason offer themselves totally to the work.' If Abraham had had a minimum of judgement he would not have pitted 318 men against an endless multitude.

But here the account highlights a second aspect of Abraham's strange behaviour. For whom is Abraham plunging in so recklessly, with almost insane bravery, risking his own and his men's life? He does it for the man who had taken the best land from him, the one who had diddled him. Had this person been honest, he would have told Abraham: you are the older man, so thanks for the offer, but you choose and I will take whatever you give me. This is the exchange of courtesies we might normally expect in such situations, yet Lot benefited from the moment of generosity and took the better land. And here is Abraham risking life and limb for this lad who ultimately has abused his kindness. Abraham is reckless, but he saves Lot and all his possessions and, as it appears from the text, without demanding anything from him. He did not say: Now come and serve me once more and don't act like you did earlier. Don't go off on your own. Let's make a single team and I will be in charge. Can't you see, you cannot manage on your own? He gives him back everything, gives him complete freedom as before.

If we read the entire chapter we also come to know from the following verses that Abraham not only freed Lot but also the king of Sodom where Lot lived. Abraham was incredibly generous with the king of Sodom too. This is the famous passage often badly translated following the Vulgate's '*da mihi animas et cetera tolle*' or 'give me souls and take all the rest.' The king of Sodom said to Abraham: 'Give me the persons but take the goods for yourself.' In other words, you have done great things for us so share the booty justly. But Abraham told the king of Sodom: 'I have sworn to the LORD, God most High, maker of heaven and earth, that I would not take a thread or a sandal thong or anything that is yours, so that you might not say, "I have made Abram rich."'

Abraham shows how truly magnanimous he is

Here, we see Abraham's whole soul, his incredible freedom of spirit, generosity, and desire to be in debt only to God. We ask ourselves what allowed Abraham such courage to overcome his fears and reason which was telling him that it was crazy to be pursuing such a powerful enemy.

What allowed Abraham to overcome his natural resentment towards Lot? He could have said – He got what he wanted! He made the choice so let him suffer the consequences. What enabled Abraham's detachment even from the booty he had won? He could have kept it, so why did he detach himself from it?

The text does not say, but the context allows us to understand, especially vv. 22-33 where Abraham says: 'I have sworn to the LORD, God Most High, creator of heaven and earth... so that you might not say, "I have made Abram rich"'. For Abraham, his wealth is Yahweh, the promise, the kerygma. He has such wealth in land, a future, Yahweh with him as a friend. As you know, throughout the Islamic tradition Abraham is called 'the friend', *el khalil*, the friend *par excellence.* Even the city of Hebron, where Abraham is buried, is called the city of the friend. Compared to this friendship with Yahweh, everything else for Abraham counts for little. He compares this wealth to the somewhat ambiguous ties that could have bound him to Sodom. The text probably wants us to note that Abraham has nothing to do with what will happen to Sodom later, and that this independence of his will be very useful, since it means he will lose nothing when Sodom is destroyed. He kept his hands clean when maybe everyone was urging him to take something, at least a minimum, something for his allies.

Abraham is a man with his feet firmly planted because he says immediately 'I will take nothing but what the young men have eaten, and the share of the men who went with me – Aner, Eschcol and Mamre. Let them take their share.' His is really a renunciation but with just consideration of others.

Abraham is not inconsiderate, thinks of others, the rights of others and keeps only his friendship with God for himself.

Here, then, are some of the effects of the kerygma in Abraham. This is why, in recalling the significance of the meditations in the Second Week, I have stressed that the retreatant, enriched by a knowledge of Christ, feels gradually freed from the decisive power of inordinate attachments: resentment, fear, greed, stinginess, niggardliness, envy, small acts of revenge, and frees himself not through the purgative way as in the First Week, but through the wealth that Christ leads to inwardly.

2. The effects of the kerygma on us Christians

Moving across to the New Testament, here are two simple examples among others of the effects of the kerygma on the Christian, so we can understand these, based on the story of Abraham, clarify their significance and see what it says to us. The examples are the two shortest parables found in all the New Testament, a verse each, the parables of the treasure hidden in the field (Mt 13:44) and the parable of the pearl (Mt 13:45-46). They are the last two before the parable of the net, concluding the parables of the Kingdom; the last one is the eschatological parable.

> The kingdom of heaven is like a treasure hidden in a field, which someone found and hid; then in his joy he goes and sells all that he has and buys that field.

We note that the man is full of joy, that is, he has the kerygma which is unexpected wealth for him. It does him good and fills him. What does he do? His action is almost feverish. We can imagine him racing home and telling his wife: quick, get the money out, call that friend I wanted to sell that field to, and the wife says: are you crazy? What are you doing? She begins to think ill of him – if you need money then maybe you have been gambling and have debts to pay, or maybe it's all gone into drugs.

But he continues: go to the other friend who owes me money and get him to give it to you immediately. Our man no longer worries about what others say or suspect (Why does he want to sell? Why does he need so much money? Maybe it's some shady affair?). Well, let them say it, because he knows that in the end he will be right, since he has this hidden treasure. It will justify everything. Clearly, he sells up everything because the treasure will be his justification.

What is the 'treasure' for us?

Here, we could make some reflections concerning ourselves: What is it that allows me to act with freedom in difficult circumstances, with constancy in weighty situations? Is it a sense of duty, the fact that we need to do things, that by now we have taken a certain direction and honesty demands we move on? Or the fact that others expect this of me and I cannot disappoint them, or that they don't expect this from me so I cannot do it? Or, is it the joy of the Kingdom, the kerygma?

It is clear that these other reasons have some significance but only within the framework of the kerygma. Removed from that they could be hypocrisy, the need for pleasure, fear of displeasing, a desire for a certain standing in life, social status, not disappointing someone else's expectations. Here is the clear and decisive fundamental meaning of the kerygma; the joy of the gospel is at the root of everything.

But we still ask ourselves what kind of joy this is. We know well that in no way is it an artificial, noisy sort of joy. In fact, sometimes it is barely perceptible, can be immersed in bitterness, but fundamentally it is there, because if it were not we would no longer be who we are as Christians. This is why it is important to understand what my kerygma is, where I see it, feel it, because it is the root of everything, all the other actions, all the other things, other choices. It is the place where God touches us in faith, God's revelation to us of himself in the intimacy of ourselves, in his trinitarian mystery of the Father who gives us the Son. This is the kerygma *par excellence*. This is why St Ignatius always points us to Christ, the Son of the Father, who is the fundamental kerygma in such a way as to make possible the other choices without letting ourselves be determined by what is negative, selfish, heavy or even senseless.

A further question: What is the strength that allows me to act in difficult circumstances? What kind of joy is this gospel joy? Is this gospel joy compatible with wisdom according to Qoheleth? This question I have already put to myself and I have still found no answer.

What is the wisdom according to Qoheleth? It is the wisdom of the one who says there is nothing new on earth, everything will be as before; things come and things go, so why bother to wear oneself out? A generation comes, a generation goes, but the earth remains the same; the sun rises, the sun sets and hastens to the place where it will rise; the wind blows to the south and goes around to the north, round and round goes the wind. That is the experience of someone who has seen many things and ultimately discovers there is not much that is new.

What relationship does all this have with gospel joy? Ecclesiastes is also an inspired book: how do we keep the two things together? It is certainly a serious problem insofar as I think that, as each of us goes through life, we come closer to these statements of Qoheleth. Things don't change much, so why get so upset about it? Then what significance does the joy of the gospel have; the novelty, involvement and risk of the gospel? It is a question we need to put to ourselves.

Finally, a reflection that might sound a bit odd: the effects of the kerygma on Jesus. It is clear that properly speaking we cannot talk about the effects of the kerygma on Jesus. Jesus is the kerygma. But we can ask how Jesus shows the kerygma in himself. To answer this question, I suggest two passages which are interesting as a comparison with texts on Abraham. One is Philippians 2:5 ff.: 'Let the same mind be in you that was in Christ Jesus, who, though he was in the form of God, did not regard equality with God as something to be exploited.' Compare this with

Abraham. While being very rich, superior to Lot, and even being able to do whatever he liked with him, in a way, Abraham did not consider his wealth and superiority to be an inalienable treasure, but stripped himself of it and let Lot make his choice. As kerygma, as gospel, Jesus displays a joyful readiness to give of himself. We cannot believe that self-giving was a sacrifice for Jesus, a burdensome duty. It is the fully available wealth of the Father that is given, the gospel experienced totally – the gospel *par excellence*, the quintessence of the gospel – the gift of the Father's love, God as love given.

Indeed, here I would like to go further and offer a critique of St Paul's text in the version quoted, where it says 'though he was in the form of God.' The 'though' here is not in the Greek, which only says 'he was in the form of God.' Why put a contrast between the fact of being of divine nature (God) and his stripping himself of that nature? I would rather say: being so rich he found the joy and fullness of giving in this richness of his. Clearly, there is a degree of contrast in the sentence: 'did not regard equality with God as something to be exploited.' But what needs to be stressed is that he could do this thanks to his richness. Hence, the kerygma provides a richness, the richness of God as love that gives of itself.

Where there is freedom, love can bud forth

A similar passage is found in 2 Corinthians 8:9, where Paul is speaking about collections: 'For you know the generous act of Our Lord Jesus Christ, that though he was rich,' (here too the Greek has a simple particle: being rich,) 'yet for your sakes he became poor, so that by his poverty you might become rich.' He wanted to make himself poor because he was rich, and being rich became poor. There is a mystery to grasp here. I recall what Romano Guardini wrote in his final work before his death, *Theological Letter to a Friend.* In the first of these letters he says: 'I am thinking at length on a mystery of God which I dare not express because it seems to me easy to misunderstand it, however, it tells me so many things about everything I have been able to see in the light of his mystery throughout my life.' And then he expounds on this concept that is difficult to express, that because he has everything, God, who is infinite, in some way seeks the finite that he does not have.

It is a thought that could be misunderstood as emanationism, but the idea is this: God's infinite richness is the foundation of his ability to make himself poor. The richness of the kerygma communicated is the foundation of our independence, our freedom, and hence of our capacity to operate according to truth and justice: all things that fundamentally require freedom and independence deep in our heart. I also invite you to meditate on this.

We can also recall St Ignatius' 'third degree of humility' which is so difficult, so I dare not speak of it because I find it so grand and lofty. But I do note that it is suggested precisely at the moment of contemplation when the retreatant is by now enriched by the fullness of Christ and so can understand it, otherwise it would look like a kind of spiritual masochism, a heroic act. Instead, the reality is that when we are rich with the fullness of Christ, when we understand Christ in his fullness, then God's love is perfect and we can give ourselves freely and also empty ourselves in this giving.

As Psalm texts I suggest Psalm 62 (63 in the Hebrew version): 'My hope is from him.' The desire for God, God who fills us with himself, allows us freedom for other things, allows us to practise justice towards matters that concern us, things around us.

When the word penetrates deeply

Finally, a text I would somewhat boldly call 'the gospel for an international community' in Luke 8:19-21:

> Then his mother and his brothers came
> to him, but they could not reach
> him because of the crowd. And he
> was told, 'Your mother and your brothers
> are standing outside, wanting to see you.'
> But he said to them, 'My mother and my
> brothers are those who hear the word of
> God and do it.'

Why have I given the passage this strange title? Because I believe it reflects very well the everyday experience in an international community: different origins, nationalities, languages, cultures, upbringing, things that are irretrievably different. People don't change, are not born anew, do not become children again to recommence an upbringing or a culture to make it homogeneous.

Now the problem is this: despite these differences, is it possible to have deeper bonds? The gospel tells us that there are even deeper bonds than upbringing and family relationships. These are the bonds of hearing the word of God and putting it into practice. This text is the basis of the possibility, the only real possibility, of creating Christian communities beyond cultural, social, environmental values, and it is also important to come together, compare ourselves with one another, try to approach the others, make ourselves permeable to others' values. It is possible up to certain point. We need to recognise that differences are part of human nature and will always exist. So, will Christian unity never exist? No, says Jesus. Something even more perfect will – and this is his promise – on the basis of hearing the word and putting it into practice. That is the dynamic of God's word; the word not merely heard, not merely echoed, but brought into decisions and choices, creates bonds of similarity, of much greater fellowship than what existed between Jesus and his brothers, even Jesus and his Mother.

We find this idea in the Koran in another form. Some years ago one of the Islamic Muftis, speaking about Bible study, told me: 'Here is what the Prophet says: "Knowledge makes those who practise it friends,"' meaning knowledge, study of the Koran, deep understanding of the word, brings friendship and fellowship to those who live by this word. This is the only real foundation of the Christian community. On this basis each one can compare ideas, thoughts, mentalities, cultures which are mutually enriching. But the roots of this community lie in the kerygma.

SIXTH MEDITATION
Abraham's state of prayer: prayer, struggle, theology

When looking through Abraham's public life for something that corresponds to Jesus' public life, I did not find much. It is true that more than once Abraham is called a prophet. Thus in Psalm 105:15, 'do not touch my anointed ones; do my prophet no harm,' also alluding to Abraham. Then there is the episode with Abimelech, king of Gerar, Genesis 20:7 to whom God says: 'Now then, return the man's wife; for he is a prophet and he will pray for you, and you shall live.' Here, Abraham is presented as a prophet, and his function as prophet is prayer.

But if we look for other prophetic activities in Abraham's life, like we find in Jesus' life, 'a great prophet in word and deed,' we find that Abraham is great in neither word nor deed. He is not great in works, nor miracles. He is not great in words because he almost never speaks. No sermon of Abraham's has been handed down to us. He gave no replies to controversial questions like Jesus did, no ready wise words.

Abraham, man of few words

Abraham remains almost always silent; he speaks two or three times. As we have seen, he speaks when he needs to be cunning. For example, in Genesis 12:11-13, when he has to convince his wife to say she is his sister. In fact, then he makes a fairly extensive speech, one of Abraham's longest. Another occasion is the similar episode involving Abimelech. He says very little – except when it suits him. So, he does speak a lot with Sarah, and again has much to say when buying the cave at Machpelah, showing what an excellent businessman he was. He also speaks when he wants to show generosity, for example when he refuses the king of Sodom's offer, and when he meets Melchisedek.

Few words of Abraham have been handed down, then. We cannot say he was a prophet in words, or that he left particular teachings, nothing like the Gospel parables or the Sermon on the Mount. Nothing! Abraham is a great man of silence, moving through different stages, at least as it seems from the text, meditating in silence. Nevertheless, there is one precise similarity between Abraham's life and that of Jesus, and it is prayer. Jesus prays, Abraham prays. Hence, I have seized upon this aspect which allows us to contemplate some scenes of Abraham as a background to the '*via illuminativa*' of Jesus.

Jesus' prayer, Abraham's prayer

There is no need to recall many texts on Jesus' prayer. I will mention two characteristics.

One is in Mark 1:35; after the busy day at Capharnaum, when he would have been really exhausted and while all the others were still asleep: 'In the morning, while it was still very dark, he got up and went out to a deserted place, and there he prayed.' Here is a typical factor in Jesus' public life: praying alone at night.

Another significant passage is Luke 5:15-16. As we know, Luke records many other passages on Jesus at prayer, but I mention this one since it serves as a point of reference. There is a contrast between verse 15: 'But now more than ever the word about Jesus spread abroad, many crowds would gather to hear him and be cured of their diseases', and the verse that follows: 'But he would withdraw to deserted places and pray.' Hence, there is a contrast between this possibility of outward apostolic success offered to Jesus, and Jesus who withdraws. Prayer is certainly an important characteristic of Jesus' mission as prophet and Messiah which we can bear in mind. In fact if someone wants to, he could meditate on these and some others I will give on prayer in Jesus' life as far as Gethsemane. But I would rather reflect with you on Abraham's prayer.

I want to say immediately that Abraham's states of prayer, especially the second and third, are difficult to understand in my view. I myself have struggled and would say that von Rad's commentary helped me a lot. I will quote him occasionally. The reason is this: they are not beginner's prayers, not easy prayers. Abraham's prayers are prayers in a situation where the understanding of God is very refined, profound, almost dangerous, meaning that

Abraham's states of prayer, especially the second and third, are those of a mature man, involved and responsible, socially committed. He bears the burdens of others, feels the destiny of his people weighing on him. It is the prayer of a leader, someone responsible, a priest. It is the prayer of a man who has responsibility and hence has a boldness, zeal, sometimes even an impudence that would sound strange in a beginner's prayer. Abraham's prayer also assumes a crisis of faith, a maturing of faith, and dark times of faith. So this prayer is not a model for beginner's prayer.

1. Prayer of listening

With this preamble, then, I will examine three typical states of Abraham's prayer.

I will not spend long on the first because it is too obvious, even though it can qualify as prayer in the broad sense. As we have said, Abraham almost never speaks, and even in his prayer there are mostly very few words, except for one case we will look at. So, Abraham listens. The first great activity of Abraham the pray-er is to listen. God speaks, repeats himself, and Abraham listens and goes, listens and moves, listens and walks. I think this is the typical, fundamental circumstance that explains all the others. If Abraham can be so bold, almost shameless, petulant and even apparently mercenary in his prayer, it is because he is first of all a very reverent listener of the word, a man who has banked his life on the word and lives by it. He listens to God's word and puts it into practice. This is the gospel ideal behind those who claim familiarity with Jesus. The true children of Abraham are those who hear the word of God and put it into practice. I will not dwell on this because it is the case throughout Abraham's life.

2. Prayer of complaint, lament

I will spend time with two other kinds of prayer, more specific kinds we will find in particular passages. The second state of prayer is, in inverted commas, 'complaint'. I call it this because it has many similarities with the Psalms of lament which take up this theme and develop it further. I would also call this prayer of lament one of questioning because it is often based on a question: Why, Lord, why are you doing this? Why do you not come to my aid? Why are you abandoning me? How come?

Two typical questions: Why? How? We find the first in Genesis 15:2:

> 'Do not be afraid, Abram, I am
> your shield; your reward shall
> be very great.' But Abram said
> 'O Lord GOD, what will you
> give me, for I continue childless,
> and the heir of my house is
> Eliezer of Damascus?'

Or in other words, Abraham is saying: Say something, Lord, explain to me why you are telling me this if my life is to continue like this.

It is clearer in v. 8, in the question: Lord God, you keep speaking about this land, but 'how am I to know I shall possess it?' We note that his prayer is the prayer of someone who has heard God's word. It is not the prayer of an unbeliever who says: how can this happen? It is a 'how can that be' of Mary's kind, not Zachariah's. The same question can be put from different points of view and have different resonances. Nevertheless, it is certainly a question that comes from within and is painful.

Then in Genesis 17:16 ff. we have a painful, even bitter question when God tells Abraham:

> 'I will bless her (Sarah) and moreover
> I will give you a son by her.
> I will bless her and she shall give
> rise to nations. Kings of peoples
> shall come from her.' Then Abraham
> fell on his face and laughed
> and said to himself, 'Can a child
> be born to a man who is a hundred
> years old? Can Sarah, who is
> ninety years old, bear a child?'
> And Abraham said to God, 'O that
> Ishmael might live in your sight!'

Here is the prayer of lament: Lord, don't go so far, I am happy with less. You promise seas and mountains but just leave me be, give me the health and strength I need now. Help me now.

This is a prayer of lament, the prayer of a man being tested, and Abraham is that man struggling with God, the man who does not understand what is happening, either to himself or others. We can often also pray like this: Lord, why are things happening like this? Why are we working so hard at the apostolate trying to build something up and it seems like it's all going to ruin? This is the big question the Psalms expand on in the history of Israel: Why do evildoers triumph and why are good oppressed? This prayer of lament can be misunderstood as a beginner's prayer. It can be a prayer of someone with little faith. In my opinion, for Abraham, instead, it is the payer of someone who feels the need, the drive to penetrate God's plan more. It is the 'how can this be?' of Mary, which in her is the highest level of closeness to God, but in Abraham is already a level of friendship.

He is provoked by the gap between promise and deeds

We could mention many Psalms which ask 'why?' Two you could reflect on are Psalms 42 and 43: Why must I walk about mournfully because the enemy oppresses me? Why can't I remain in your house with glad shouts and songs of thanksgiving? Here I am thirsty, depressed and far from the city.

If we ask ourselves what the ultimate category is for summing up all these questions in Psalms of lament, and especially Abraham's questions, the questions of a man experiencing the ambiguity of history and questioning it in prayer, I would say that what gives rise to these questions is the gap, or at least the apparent gap, between the promise and what we see. If there were not this great promise we would be fatalists; things must go that way so let's accept them. We would say that since God reveals himself in everything, so he will reveal himself in the nothingness of my life! But there is a promise and the promise is joy, fullness, a people of God, fraternal communion among human beings. So why is it not realised?

This is the painful, and painfully felt gap for Abraham, the man of faith – the gap between the greatest of promises which is repeated, insisted upon, and the reality. Here is the origin of the prayer of lament. If prayed in a style of friendship it is an attempt (as the Psalms say, *'Donec intravi in sancta Dei*, until I went into the sanctuary of God, Ps 73:17) to enter God's sanctuary and understand him better: My God, who are you? Since your promise is real and I cannot doubt it, since the reality is so wretched and I have the evidence, then it means that I will discover the relationship between these two things in a new understanding of who you are, it means I have not understood you, that I have more to understand, and I pray that I can understand you more. I offer my suffering at not understanding you enough, because if you were as I have thought you were, you would have already realised the promise, would have already done what I asked for that person, that situation, for the world, for justice... Instead, you have not done so while still promising to. This means I have not yet understood you. So, grant that I may understand you more.

Prayer that could sound blasphemous

This is the painful prayer of someone whose familiarity with faith can achieve an even more profound familiarity, while being expressed in almost blasphemous words because it questions God (certain Psalms reach a level of violence that sounds blasphemous). This prayer from Abraham's perspective as God's friend experiences these things, yet it goes from friendship to friendship, from familiarity to familiarity. It is no beginner's prayer nurturing lack of faith or complaining as if God were being sued: I was expecting this, I started out on my spiritual life believing all my faults would disappear. Now look at me just as I was before! Why? How come?

Faith made firm by the power of the word does not exclude this lament, and indeed the Psalter is full of it, but it is a loving even if painful effort to get to know you more, O God; for you to reveal yourself this way. Why do I not understand you? Why do you not make yourself understood? Only a friend can say these things. If someone outside were to say them it would sound blasphemous, an insult to speak to God this way. But a friend like Abraham, or like the psalmist, dares much more, not just on tip-toe but with his whole being behind it.

The Psalms are full of fury, emotion. They can even be prayer of outrage. But if God inspired this prayer it means God loves emotion, outrage in friendship. God is not a cold friend. He is a God who loves this protest that seeks to understand him more deeply. We could say he prefers outrageous protestors to the resigned, indifferent ones. This is what I seem to gather by examining Abraham's state of prayer, the kind that I am calling prayer of lament.

3. Prayer of intercession

And so I come to the third characteristic, the third state, the one I call 'prayer of intercession' in inverted commas. Under this label I intend to include the famous negotiations over Sodom in Chapter 18: the lengthy dialogue God has with Abraham under the oaks of Mamre, at a decent distance from Sodom. It is a difficult passage, one which I struggled to penetrate. But as I said, von Rad's commentary helped a lot and I will read some of it. Here I also believe, as von Rad says, that it is too little to call it 'prayer of intercession'. After all, Abraham intercedes unsuccessfully for Sodom which is about to be destroyed. Abraham would still be a great intercessor, even though in this instance he lacked an adequate subject to intercede for.

In the Yahwist context, this prayer is a later addition, a theological reflection on the event. Authors note that here the redactor is much freer, not tied to traditions. He is not simply giving an account from some past tradition, but theologising. This is his theology where he develops a certain idea of God. It is an effort to gain a new understanding of God, get to know him better, shift from an understanding of the God of Ur of the Chaldeans to one of the God of salvation.

So it is a prayer we should really call a prayer of theological penetration. This is what I would call it.

Ultimately, von Rad puts it well; it is a theological page told in the dramatic form of prayer, almost as a poem. It is a prayer of theological penetration of the mystery of human affairs as God judges them. So it is a prayer over the world, society, the circumstances surrounding us. It is also a prayer of involvement because Lot is in Sodom, so Abraham is strongly involved with the place. He is not just a philosopher speculating about a corrupt city, saying: What will happen? How will God look upon it? There is an element of this but there is also a terrible involvement; Abraham is praying for his kindred.

Let us look briefly at this episode, reading it with a '*brevis et summaria declaratio*' as St Ignatius says, with some points for reflection.

The episode with Lot and family at Sodom

The text is Genesis 18:16-33. After the appearance of the 'three men' at the oaks of Mamre; after the renewed promise to Sarah, and Sarah's laughter, the text first of all describes the situation, vv. 16-20. It narrates the story of Abraham's double intervention.

What is the situation? After telling Sarah: yes, you did laugh, facing her with her error, her inability to believe:

> Then the men set out from there,
> and they looked toward Sodom;
> and Abraham went with them to
> set them on their way. The LORD
> said, 'Shall I hide from Abraham

> what I am about to do, seeing
> that Abraham shall become a great
> and mighty nation, and all the
> nations of the earth shall be blessed
> in him? No, for I have chosen him,
> that he may charge his children
> and his household after him to
> keep the way of the Lord by doing
> righteousness and justice, so that
> the Lord may bring about for
> Abraham what he has promised him.'

Here,e the redactional composition uses already typical passages and brings them together to remind us of the privileged relationships God has with Abraham. We are probably at a later language stage rather than that of the Deuteronomist: 'I have chosen him,' meaning that Abraham is the friend, the bridegroom, the one I have deeply loved.

Then comes a first step: God, and standing before him Abraham, friend and progenitor of a great nation in the fullness of his function; the intimate friend whom nothing is hidden from – recall John 15:15: 'I have made known to you everything that I have heard from my Father' – hence the confident sharing in God's plan for history. To be truly head of a nation, Abraham must enter into God's plan, not experience it from outside as a mere spectator. He must share it intimately, understand God's plan.

Then comes a second step:

> Then the Lord said, 'How great is the
> outcry against Sodom and Gomorrah

and how very grave their sin!
I must go down and see whether
they have done altogether according
to the outcry that has come to me/
and if not I will know.'

This second moment involves the gravity of the two cities' sin. It is the typical case of those who are unjustly oppressed, live under oppression, injustice and turn to the judge. If the judge does not bring them justice, then their cry rises up to God and God must step in. This is clearly a cosmic situation: God, the one God has chosen for his people, and the world with its sin, its injustice. God will judge the world. What function will Abraham, his friend, have in this judgment of the world?

Abraham's 'legal' argument

This situation brings about a double intervention by Abraham – we say double but it is really more complex – which begins with a fundamental issue, a legal one I would call it, which is the core, the strength of Abraham's argument. This issue is expressed in vv. 23-25. Then comes a negotiation based on this matter, vv. 26-33. But first of all there is a very interesting preface to it all. 'So the men turned from there and went towards Sodom, while Abraham remained standing before the LORD' (v. 22). There is an important problem of textual criticism here. The scene has begun to become clearer from a theological perspective: the three men become two angels and the one remaining is

Yahweh with Abraham before him. The biblical text says 'While Abraham remained standing before the LORD' but a masoretic note indicates that a change has occurred here. In all probability the ancient tradition read: 'While the LORD remained standing before Abraham,' which sounds much less dignified – standing before someone implied almost serving him – so it has been reversed: 'Abraham remained standing before the LORD.' von Rad notes: 'Yahweh who wants to be questioned, wants Abraham to say something to him, to ask to be part of his plan and who stands there, in silence, ready to receive Abraham's word as he questions God, because God wants to manifest himself.'

Then comes the legal principle preceding the negotiations: 'Then Abraham came near and said, "Will you indeed sweep away the righteous with the wicked?"' The same principle is taken up once more following this: 'Far be it from you to do such a thing, to slay the righteous with the wicked so that the righteous fare the same as the wicked. Far be that from you! Shall not the judge of all the earth do what is just?' Abraham calls on a notion of justice, as we shall see, that already has a significance which goes well beyond the notions of the time.

Then the negotiation

Strengthened by this principle, Abraham then shirtfronts God: 'Suppose there are fifty righteous within the city; will you then sweep away the place and not forgive it for the fifty righteous who are in it?' Abraham is excited. He has said so much, as he does here. 'And the LORD said, "If I find at Sodom fifty righteous in the city, I will forgive the whole place for their sake."' There is a formidable leap in quality in this reply compared with the mentality of the time. Since God has accepted the legal criterion based on number, Abraham is now sure of this departure point and lowers it incrementally from 50 to 45, 45 to 40, 40 to 30, 30 to 20, 20 to 10.

This movement is interesting, because except for the case of 40, all the others are preceded by a statement of humility: '"Let me take it upon myself to speak to the LORD, I who am but dust and ashes. Suppose five of the fifty righteous are lacking? Will you destroy the whole city for lack of five?" And he said, "I will not destroy it if I find forty-five there."' He has the same reply if there are forty. Then comes the same reply if there are forty. Then comes the same question yet again: 'Then he said, "Oh, do not let the LORD be angry if I speak. Suppose thirty are found there." He answered, "I will not do it if I find thirty there."' And so on until the figure comes down to ten: "For the sake of ten I will not destroy it." The dialogue then ceases: 'And the LORD went his way, when he had finished speaking to Abraham.' We are left wondering though: why stop at 10? What happened? The reality is that Sodom is destroyed.

The significance of this episode for us

What is this whole story trying to tell us, mysterious and a little disturbing as it is? If we want to reflect on it, it should be said first of all that we are dealing with a competent, cunning negotiation. Abraham is an excellent businessman. He first ensures that the general principle is accepted. Then, bolstered by this principle, he argues by saying that the principle still holds when the number is reduced. It is not only a competent negotiation but also a dogged one. Abraham does not give in. Why? The first idea that comes to me is this: Abraham wants to get down to the number of Lot's family members; he is thinking that between Lot, his wife and some friends there are about a dozen, and he stops at this point because it would be too much to go any further. This is the obvious impression. I would say that the dialogue leaves the reader with this obvious impression. But here I will read a page from von Rad that seems very important to me because it makes us go further. He says: 'The debate, which is not without irony, turns on a serious question of faith. Here, it is completely a Yahwist theology. It is not just an ancient detail but the Yahwist who considers the relationship between God and the man he has chosen, and the world. It is not just a case of saving Sodom and Lot that is being dealt with here. Sodom is an extreme case which serves as an example to demonstrate a theological thesis. Sodom is no longer considered expressly as a city outside the people of the Covenant, as if Sodom may perish as long as Israel is saved. On the contrary, for Israel, Sodom is the type of a human community which Yahweh's gaze falls on to judge it. It is a typical case showing how Yahweh judges the world, and how Yahweh's judgement on the world comes about.'

A *sinful group of people*

Clearly, the first interpretation one could think of and which we can in some way deduce from God's words: 'How great is the outcry against Sodom and Gomorrah and how grave their sin' is the one which applies the idea of the ancient world which sees groups as a solid entity – if there is a group where the majority are sinners, then this is a sinful group because in concrete terms, personal freedom is much reduced and solidarity is extreme. All are involved. This mentality is very well expressed by Abimelech in Chapter 20:9: 'What have you done to us? How have I sinned against you, that you have brought such great guilt on me and my kingdom?' Hence, Abimelech's sin is the kingdom's sin. This solidarity is experienced in such a way that when there are many sinners in a city, the city is sinful. So, in the notion of solidarity common to the ancient world, judgement comes upon the whole city. It follows that the individual is involved in the common sin, no exceptions admitted. Everyone is part of what happens in the city and shares in its sin.

Here though, given this mentality, we already have a first step beyond it: 'Will you indeed sweep away the righteous with the wicked?' What is this first step asking? It is asking for what will flourish even more clearly in Israel: individual responsibility or, in other words, we do not condemn a city in its entirety because a large part of it has abused its power. If there are some righteous people there, let them go free because justice requires that each individual be recognised for his or her responsibility. Yet, Abraham's dialogue with

God goes much further, because in Abraham's words: 'Will you indeed sweep away the righteous with the wicked? Suppose there are fifty righteous within the city.' We are at the level of someone who says 'at least separate the fifty righteous people.'

A God who wants to save by forgiving everyone

The reply God gives goes well beyond the request! 'If I find at Sodom fifty righteous in the city I will forgive the whole place for their sake.' This is a completely new concept entering here: it is not simply a matter of separating the just from the unjust, but of giving greater weight to a few righteous people than to a multitude of sinners, and by turning solidarity into vicariousness, saving the whole city in view of a few. Clearly, this is how a new concept of justice is being established: not the justice that seeks to give each his due and separate the good from the bad, but justice that seeks to save everyone, and the righteous are used as the lever for this.

But we ask ourselves: why does Abraham stop at ten? Von Rad, too, asks himself this and says that ten seems to be an absolute minimum. For the Yahwist redactor it is not possible to go beyond that number. In fact, the solution God follows is that of personal responsibility, that is, he saves Lot the righteous one and destroys the sinful city. In this perspective it would seem to be unattainable to ask for more. It was already a huge thing for a city to be saved for ten people.

We have here the basis for a theology that will emerge in all its power in Isaiah 53: for just one righteous person God will save all the people. Hence, Abraham is struggling for a new understanding of God, the God of salvation, the God who so much wants to save that he is ready to forgive everyone because of one, and he becomes that one in order to save everyone. Here, prayer truly is struggle at the same time. This negotiation to the end is really exhausting for Abraham, and it is theology, that is, a new understanding of God which develops and is then expressed in the theology of the Yahwist.

Von Rad puts it this way: Yahweh has a relationship of communion with Sodom too. This relationship is broken by the sins of the majority of its inhabitants and also includes the few innocent ones; yet Yahweh's justice for Sodom is manifested precisely by the fact that in view of these innocent ones he will spare the city. Certainly, von Rad says, this is not expressed by Abraham in God's sight as if he were dealing with a theological proposition, but in the form of a humble request and with anguished heart. Because he is excited, many words escape his lips. Clearly, there is a struggle going on in him between the sense of respect owed to God and the urgency of the problem posed by faith. Here he quotes Jeremiah 12:1 which I believe is interesting in this context: 'You will be in the right, O Lord, when I lay charges against you; but let me put my case to you.' It is a prayer of intercession and of theological penetration: Lord, I would like to understand your justice better. He then begins with: 'Why does the way of the guilty prosper?' and then he continues with a range of questions.

Abraham becomes even more courageous

Contrary to modern man, Abraham knows well that, dust and ashes as he is, he has no right to argue with God, but it is magnificent to see how, as the conversation proceeds, and in the face of Yahweh's benevolence, he gradually gains courage and plays more boldly on the potential of a justice which does not ignore forgiveness, and he presses on until he finally obtains the surprising reply that even a tiny number of innocent people in God's eyes counts more than a majority of guilty ones. Thus, he is able to hold back the pronouncement of sentence.

We can conclude by asking: Who is Abraham? How is Abraham presented here? Abraham is God's friend, bold to the point of impudence because he wants to get to know God more profoundly, and we could almost say that he is forgiven much in this impudence because he has loved much. He wants to love God immensely and so wants to understand him and justify him in his own and the world's eyes that he puts even bolder requests to him. Abraham also struggles with God because he feels responsible before God for his nephew and the city where his nephew lives and is bound up with. He struggles with God with the same relentlessness with which he fought against the four kings with his 318 men.

Struggle and prayer. Abraham threw himself into the fight to death to save Lot, and here he throws himself into prayer almost to the point of irreverence. But he does so in the fullness of faith, to understand God's plan and to understand the basic problem of God's justice towards mankind. This is why I have linked prayer-struggle-theology in the title. Theology or an understanding of God. Through all these realities the human being tries to understand who this God of salvation is, the true God, not the one I imagine and think, but the God who acts, judges, saves.

A kind of prayer also found in the New Testament

Following on from this general proposition regarding Abraham, I am offering a second one on New Testament themes: Romans 15:30-31; 2 Corinthians 1:11; Ephesians 6:18; Colossians 4:3; 1 Thessalonians 3:10. These are very interesting texts because they speak of the dramatic appeals Paul puts to the community or his prayer for the community. Here is the same sense of responsibility that Paul has for God's plan, the shared sense of responsibility Christians have for this plan, involvement in the prayer of intercession that this plan of God's may be clear, made manifest, that the word may spread, etc. I think it could be interesting to meditate on the true prayer of intercession of the Christian, and that of Abraham, as Moses does when he says: cancel me from the book of life but save this people. And as Paul does: I would like to be anathema for the sake of my brother and sister. It is a prayer that presumes involvement, presumes the deepest affection.

It is not the simple prayer that we sometimes use for intentions: 'Lord, hear us… Lord hear our prayer,' which only involves us to some extent. Prayer for those for whom we bear serious responsibility, whose burden we have taken on, with whom we share a risk, is the prayer that leads us to this earnest, impudent penetration of God's plan. If we do not know this plan how can we ask that it be fulfilled? And we do not know it because we do not know God, so we ask to know him so that his plan may be fulfilled, his word spread, be made manifest, that the doors of the gospel may open, etc. These are all comments by prayer in this context.

To broaden the theme, we can recall the text on Jesus' prayer of intercession in Hebrews 5:7, a supplication with loud cries and tears he makes for the world. It is a text that needs to be interpreted by meditating on the agony in the garden at Gethsemane. This, too, is a very instructive text for Jesus' dramatic involvement in prayer. Finally, Psalms 42-43, among the most beautiful of the Psalms of lament: 'Why are you cast down, O my soul, and why are you disquieted within me?'

An alternative Gospel passage could be the very brief one in Luke 3:21-22 on Jesus' baptism. According to Luke, Jesus is at prayer and when Jesus prays, adoring the Father, he intercedes for the world. In this prayer, and while involving himself in our situation through his baptism, the Father reveals himself to him. I would say it is a fundamental text on Jesus' involvement in prayer, on his sharing and his solidarity with us.

Another Gospel text we could meditate on is Luke's words in Luke 11:1-13 on the urgent insistence, the importunity of prayer, the brazenness of prayer, which seems to me to reflect well what Abraham says. A further useful text to read could be Paul's prayer in 2 Corinthians 1:6-11 for a dramatic circumstance in his life, involving the community in his fears and suffering.

SEVENTH MEDITATION
Abraham's test and our trials

We praise you and we thank you,
O glorious Lord Jesus Christ,
because you are present among and in us;
you praise the Father in us perfectly
with the voice of the Spirit you have given us.
We ask you, O Lord,
that this voice of the Spirit
may be aroused in us
by listening to the words of scripture
in a dignified, just way
that is suited to the meaning of the text,
proportionate to the things it shows us,
ready to recognise in us the similarities
with the teaching and example
offered us.
You are God who lives and reigns
forever and ever. Amen.

We would like to meditate today on Abraham's trial in Genesis 22. It is the culminating text of Abraham's experience, a text, as von Rad, one of his sharpest commentators, says: 'no one can approach in a neutral way. It seems to provoke some admiration, discomfort, fear, confusion in us. It is a text we gladly avoid because it creates problems and difficulties and can also create scandal, derision. It is a text we feel we understand so little of inasmuch as it is crystal clear. It is a story from an Elohist source, almost without blemish from a purely formal literary point of view. It is without wrinkle, probably a little later in redaction, hence reflective of literary skill, a consummate ability to tell a story. There are some later additions which disturb the unity of the whole from a literary point of view, but which converge on and clarify the meaning of the episode. Nevertheless, despite its clarity, the text can appear to be disturbing, harsh, difficult. I think Luther once said: "I understand less of it than the hoof of Abraham's donkey understood while stationed at the foot of the mountain. The donkey did not climb the mountain and did not even see what was happening."'

More delicately, Kierkegaard speaks of a man who heard this story told by a child and went over it in his mind with ever greater enthusiasm, but just the same his understanding of the story became more and more difficult. He concluded with his usual irony: 'That man was not learned, was not an exegete, he did not understand Hebrew. Had he understood Hebrew, perhaps Abraham's story would have become easy for him.' But really, even someone who understands Hebrew finds this story just as difficult. So what can we do? We will very simply do what St Ignatius says to do: offer the story as is, *'cum brevi vel summaria declaratione'* (add only a short or summary explanation)

[2], with some pointers for interpretation. So first, we will make a brief analysis of the text, its structure, then we will say something on the many interpretations of the story and finish with some concluding reflections.

1. Abraham's test: analysis of the text

What does Abraham's test consist of? What tests do we face? If we want to frame the reflections I am about to offer you within the dynamics of this retreat, we need to remind ourselves of what we were saying on day one: What understanding of God did Abraham start out with? Abraham started with an astrological understanding, certainly an imperfect one, of a God who can be managed, whom we obtain favours from through rites. We can see where this God goes or doesn't go by looking at the stars. It is a God we are sure of in some way, who makes our life secure because we can count on him, because he is as regular as the stars.

Now we see that Abraham gradually shifts from a God he can count on and manage, to a God who manages him, does so continuously with increasingly subtler and more difficult tests interspersed with promise. He refines this understanding of himself and leads him to the God of promise, the God he needs to lean on entirely, totally, uniquely, the God who has his life's destiny in his hands, who knows him. But Abraham does not see the concrete fulfillment of the promises, and the understanding he had previously acquired through so much effort seems to burst through once more.

Here is the episode: Abraham had believed he had understood something more about God: it is the God of promise, the God who leads him, even if he does not see where; the God who is preparing a land for him and a people, and finally, a son. He is the God of kindness, justice, truth, fullness. But it seems that at a certain point all this is thrown into question. A new leap is required in his understanding of God.

The four elements of the text

The text of Genesis 22:1-18 comprises four parts:

(vv. 1-2) *The command.* The first part is the command: 'After these things God tested Abraham,' God is once more the actor as he was in Genesis 12: 'God called Abraham.' The account is established theologically this way from the outset, and we note that the redactor seems to immediately want to involve us in the action because he tells us what is happening: 'God tested Abraham. He said to him, "Abraham!" And he said, "Here I am."' He said, "Take your son, your only son Isaac, whom you love, and go to the land of Moriah, and offer him there as a burnt offering on one of the mountains that I shall show you."' Here is the command. In its clarity the account is almost completely devoid of emotional elements, almost a photograph detached from events except for some hints that let us foresee the drama: 'your son, your only son, whom you love.'

(vv. 3-6, 9-12). *The execution of the command.* The execution of the command is described at length. The narrator loves to go on at length; he seems to want to stress that Abraham took a few days when it would have been easier to do everything immediately. Instead no, there are preparations, a silent journey, a heavy atmosphere, no one daring to ask: Where are we going? All this is indirectly described by the narrator, slowing things down: 'So Abraham rose early in the morning,' hence he did not hesitate an instant in carrying out the Lord's command which he probably received at night, 'saddled his donkey, and took two of his young men with him, and his son Isaac; he cut the wood for the burnt offering and set out and went to the place in the distance that God had shown him.' Note the details: saddling the donkey, cutting the wood, taking the servants. The author insists on minimal, almost banal details in contrast to the drama unfolding and which none of the actors in the story dares talk about. The commentators' imagination runs wild at this point: Would Sarah have known, not known, or understood? Some describe her watching out the window. There is nothing of this in the story. Anything sentimental has been discarded.

'On the third day Abraham looked up and saw the place far away.' Implicitly it is saying here that the journey lasted three days and three nights, so this means setting up camp each evening, rising in the morning and setting out again, etc. 'Then Abraham said to his young men, "Stay here with the donkey; the boy and I will go over there; we will worship and then we will come back to you."' Abraham understands that something unheard of is to happen between himself and God. He does not want witnesses, not even the donkey. No one must be there; no one should see what will happen.

(vv. 7-8). *The conversation.* Then follows the conversation between Abraham and Isaac. It is the culminating moment of the dramatic action when the most intimate family ties come into play: 'Isaac said to his father Abraham, "Father!" And he said, "Here I am my son." He said, "The fire and wood are here, but where is the lamb for a burnt offering?" Abraham said, "God himself will provide the lamb for a burnt offering, my son."' It is a masterpiece of dialogue where so much is implied but where Isaac's simplicity, which looks to the essential, contrasts with Abraham's embarrassment. He also looks to the essential: God will provide! Finally (vv. 9-10) we have the preparation for the sacrifice: 'So the two of them walked on together. And when they came to the place that God had shown him,' and here the action slows down again, 'Abraham built an altar there and laid the wood in order. He bound his son Isaac, and laid him on the altar, on top of the wood. Then Abraham reached out his hand and took the knife to kill his son.' The preparation for the sacrifice is told in minute detail.

(vv. 11-14). *The oath repeated.* In the last part of the text comes the oath once more: 'The angel of the Lord called to Abraham a second time from heaven and said, "By myself I have sworn, says the Lord: Because you have done this, and have not withheld your son, your only son, I will indeed bless you, and I will make your offering as numerous as the stars of heaven and as the sand that is on the seashore. And your offspring shall possess the gate of their enemies, and by your offspring shall all the nations of the earth gain blessings for themselves, because you have obeyed my voice."' Note that for the third time it insists on 'your only son'.

'Abraham then returned to his young men and they arose and went together to Beersheba, and Abraham lived at Beersheba' (v. 19).

One commentator notes: no word of joy, exultation, enthusiasm; all in a subdued tone. One rabbinical commentator says that when Isaac returned home he recounted everything to his mother Sarah who cried out six times then died! Commentators always like to expand on things, see what lies behind them, the feelings disturbing the souls of individuals. But the text says nothing of this. By considering the text as a whole, we see that it is all placed within a very clear theological frame. Verse 1: 'God tested Abraham'; verse 126: 'now I know that you fear God, since you have not withheld your son, your only son, from me.' This is the theological frame for the test, almost like a stress test for a building, to see if it is able to withstand these forces.

Within this theological frame we find the story with two strictly contradictory elements. Verse 2: 'Take your son, your only son… Offer him there as a burnt offering'; verse 12: 'Do not lay your hand on the boy or do anything to him.' The centre of the account is found between these two commands. Then there is a sentence repeated twice with two different meanings; verse 8: 'God himself will provide the lamb for a burnt offering, my son'; then again in verse

14: 'So Abraham called that place "The LORD will provide" as it is said to this day, "On the mount of the LORD it shall be provided."' This sentence, first uttered amid his confusion with bitterness, then later with clarity, seems to me to express the crucial point around which all the other themes of Abraham's tests are organised.

2. Interpretation of the text

Let us say a word about interpretations. I have already mentioned the *rabbinical* ones. Right back since ancient times this story has attracted commentators because of its human and religious dramatic nature: a father who wants to kill his son in order to obey God – the worst of crimes committed out of the best of duties. It is a religious drama told without comment, almost devoid of psychological, emotional and theological indications, and this very fact has led to a heap of reflections. They take it up with their own meanings and relive it according to their own religious experiences. It is clear that we are dealing with an extreme case which implies a leap in quality, a leap in Abraham's level of experience in his understanding of God.

Among these interpretations are some *soft* ones which tend to de-dramatise the account. They say that the purpose of the text is to demonstrate that God does not want human sacrifices. But they have a rather crude way of demonstrating it. From an archaeological perspective it is said that the text points to an ancient tradition of human sacrifice at the founding of shrines, and here it points to the Hebrews who began not to do this. But although in archaeological terms we can make reference to the story's prehistory, the text makes no mention of places of worship or at least not clearly so, except for the proverbial saying: 'On the mount of the LORD it shall be provided'.

According to another soft interpretation, Abraham erred, meaning he believed God was asking him to sacrifice his son. He had seen Canaanite human sacrifices, and believing there was something heroic about them, told himself he had to do the same. He made a mistake until God enlightened him. But we can ask ourselves: Why not enlighten him earlier? Why let him come to this point? They are all interpretations trying to read the text according to a later perspective, and they can have some plausibility.

Opposed to these soft interpretations are some rather *hard* ones which insist on faith, faith in absurdity. Although it might seem too simple a way to sum these up, I think Kierkegaard expresses these hard interpretations well when he speaks of the need for faith as a condition for surpassing earlier understanding, for a suspension of the ethical because it is imposed upon by the religious: the drama by which judgement on what seems ethically reasonable, just, dutiful, or ethically macabre and unjust, as in the killing of a child, is suspended before a higher instance.

Sarcastic interpretations

The interpretations falling between the soft and the hard are the *sarcastic* ones. Von Rad recalls one by Kolacowski, a Polish Marxist living in London, who tells the story in a humorous, sarcastic tone, even though with some profound insight. For him, Abraham represents obedience to the State. Abraham does this very well: one must never question an order, which must be followed in every case. So Abraham is the model of the perfect citizen who always obeys the laws. Abraham perfectly held to what was commanded of him and so did not sin. He neither wanted to kill Isaac nor hold back. Ultimately, behind this story is a parody of obedience to the State's way of thinking, which in the end becomes a parody of the concept of God.

I tell you this to show how the story has a whole range of applications and can also be a strong point for the non-believer who, in the face of this account, finds the concept of God inadmissible, a God who creates fear and gives us the shivers. We never succeed in completely exhausting the meaning of this story, and can never say we have fully understood it. Every time, there is a need to try to see what the narrator wanted to say. Its interpretation has been constantly probed further, especially in the modern era, for its individualistic, ethical, psychological aspects. People have sought to understand what Abraham thought, what he told Isaac, if he told him what he was preparing to do, or if he told him nothing.

I refer to another observation of Kierkegaard's on these questions: Abraham did not speak to Isaac about it. He preferred to be considered his son's killer than for his son to lose faith, because had he explained it to him, his son would not have understood. It is one of the many psychological complications we have to deal with if we go beyond the text which in itself remains very simple, detached.

What does the Scripture say?

With so many interpretations, what do we do? I will simply offer some reflections, first of all about Abraham's text, and then ours, which we know better than Abraham's. We were not on Mount Moriah, so we cannot know exactly what this test of Abraham really represented, not according to suggestions of imagination, psychology, and deep exploration of the psyche. But what does the Scripture say?

The Scripture clearly says at verse 12: 'Now I know that you fear God', hence we know it is a test, a test that touches Abraham in his depths, in his relationship with God, in his relationship of obedience and faith. It is not simply a test on the cardinal virtues of justice, fortitude, temperance like other earlier texts could be, for example in Egypt where his loyalty was on trial, and his fortitude – he failed; or when he and Lot separated, where the text was on temperance with regard to his possessions – and he passed. Here it is a deeper test, a test on fear of God, on how Abraham accepts the God of salvation, the God of free initiative and promise which his life by now depends on.

Beyond this significance, the Scriptures offer many other broader ones. For example, in 1 Macabees 2:52: 'Was not Abraham found faithful when tested, and it was reckoned to him as righteousness?' In other translations, it refers to Abraham remaining faithful in temptation, which I would think means he never tired of obedience in faith, but persevered in this obedience even when it became almost impossible. Other better known passages insist mainly on faith as such. For example, Hebrews 11: 17-19: 'By faith

Abraham, when put to the test, offered up Isaac. He who had received the promises was ready to offer up his only son, of whom he had been told, "It is through Isaac that descendants shall be named for you." He considered the fact that God is able even to raise someone from the dead – and figuratively speaking, he did receive him back.' Here the insistence is on the central object of Abraham's faith and the promise: descendants. Abraham is tempted regarding the central object of the promise given him, and he accepts this test.

Again in Hebrews 6:15, the insistence is on perseverance: 'And thus Abraham, having patiently endured, obtained the promise.' Other texts, instead, insist on the obedient execution of God's command. Thus, James 2:21: 'Was not our ancestor Abraham justified by works when he offered his son Isaac on the altar?' James is underscoring the fact of obedience in itself, the execution of obedience as such, while Hebrews, it seems to me, is underscoring the intention with which Abraham obeys. The Book of Wisdom 10:5 emphasises Abraham's fortitude, hence a temptation regarding the cardinal virtues: 'Wisdom recognised the righteous man and kept him blameless before God, and kept him strong in the face of his compassion for his child.' As you can see, there are various nuances in the Scriptures, various accents taken from these texts. What are we to say? Simply, without seeking to provide any profound exegesis, we should exclude modern interpretations of the text as not fully pertinent, especially from Kierkegaard onwards. Of themselves they are quite fascinating when they recall the concept of surpassing ethics and the conflict of duties: man caught between two duties, the duty of preserving his son, and the duty of obeying God's voice telling him to kill him. This conflict of duties which really disturbs us moderns does not seem to me to appear in the Israelite mindset. We recall that in ancient civilisations, including in Roman times, the father held the right of life and death over the child. However, it does not seem to me that this ethical conflict appears in the text and is not emphasised by the text's mindset. It is our mindset. It insists rather on a conflict of tenderness, love, but not between two opposing laws or between two opposing things God wants, which tears the soul apart. It does not seem to me to be the case that surpassing, overcoming the ethical plane corresponds to the author's theology, because there is no basic ethical problem posed.

The human being faced with limits

So, what can we say positively about Abraham's action? It seems to me it is simply this: Abraham's test, like any serious test, is one of the human being faced with an extreme situation where the individual shows who he or she truly is. It is a bit like Job: brought to the limit, Job shows who he is. What is the limit for Abraham? He is provoked to a point of almost *absolute* impossibility because, as the letter to the Hebrews says (Heb 11:9): Abraham believed in resurrection, even if there is something of a New Testament anticipation in this. However, it is certainly a provocation to the point of improbability, something too difficult to be accepted by Abraham's faith. Abraham's faith is stretched to the limit.

If we want Abraham to speak with God without too much psychology, very simply he would say: Well then, to put it briefly, you have promised so much, I have waited so long, and finally you have given me a beginning to the nation you promised me, a necessary beginning, because we cannot start without this. You have given me this and I have him with me as a sign of your kindness, as hope for my future, the pledge that you are my God, and now you are telling me to take this means away. So what will become of me? There could only be questions of this kind arising in Abraham, whose faith is being tested to the extreme: Who is this God who seems to contradict himself? Who is this God who has brought me so far, whom I seemed to discern correctly and now he wants me to do the opposite? We see that I never understand him. Or is it I who am submerged in a sea of religious scruples?

But Abraham did not come to this point. It is us moderns who arrive there. Nevertheless, the limit which this test is, does lie here, I believe. It really is a test of faith, a test of faith which involves the promise. It not only involves tenderness for a son but the whole of the posterity promised him in this son. Abraham has this small pledge whereby he sees God's blessing, and now it is to be taken from him. So where is God's blessing? What will become of him? I believe, from the Bible's point of view, that this is the way we can somehow interpret the extreme situation Abraham is brought to.

Our tests

Following this first reflection, let me offer another on our own tests. Certainly this test was given Abraham for the whole people of Israel who would look at it forever as a test for all men and women who refer themselves to Abraham and are contained within him. Abraham's test is ours too in some way. So first of all, I suggest as an introduction that we ask ourselves: What are my tests? I will then suggest three brief ideas on our tests, starting from the theme of Abraham.

Let us reflect a little on our tests first of all, 'our' meaning as individuals, community, collectively – socially and as Church. They are all tests that affect us. We not only have mysterious, hidden personal trials, but also ones where we are associated with others close to us by reason of apostolate, vocation, apostolic mission, affection, etc., just as we are also associated with the rest of humanity. I invite you to reflect on these trials just as we have reflected on our kerygmas, our gospels, and to reflect especially on tests of our deepest attitude which are the tests found in Genesis 22.

We too have tests of the kind found in Genesis 12 or Genesis 22, which might only indirectly touch on our deepest attitude to God, our image of God. For example, an unpleasant duty we have to carry out can be difficult, but it is not yet a test which touches us in the very intimacy of our being. Similarly, an illness which is troubling and difficult can take some effort to overcome, but it does not yet go to the heart of things. Or there might be some unpleasant circumstances: we might cut a bad figure, make a costly mistake. These are all tests but they touch on the cardinal virtues like fortitude, prudence, temperance. They can be tests of chastity, temptations of various kinds which touch on these virtues, but they still do not touch the intimacy of our attitude to God.

The test that throws our faith into confusion

There are tests, instead, that as Paul would say, are like flaming arrows launched by the enemy which tend to strike at what is the very identity of our faith and reach into our intimate self. They can come from major events but even very simple ones which as typical and symbolic events frighten us, throw us into confusion because we see in them a whole situation, a system which dominates us. I would describe this kind of test as a painful and threatening perception of the gap between the divine promise and reality. It is a perception which leaves us shaken and we start to waver. At this point we are in Abraham's situation.

What brings this about? We are tempted by questions that arise. How come? If this is how it is, why does God not intervene? Is God not our Father? Is Christ not really alive in his Church? How come things are going like this? Where is all God's concern for mankind? And a thousand other questions that touch the core of our religious identity. These tests can be both physical and moral. Certain endless agonies, torturous deaths which force us to see the absence of God. God does not come to our aid and allows an individual to deteriorate through suffering – maybe people we have loved, followed, who have lived a life of faith with us and we see them fail. Why? How does all this come about? There may be situations of injustice where innocent people suffer: Why does God not intervene?

This is the problem of evil which is the common denominator in all objections to God. If your God really does exist, why does he allow this, that or the other? The list is endless and not only in the area of worldly experiences, the realities of this world, but also in the Church: slowness, scandal, hypocrisy, apostolic works that seem promising but are then ruined by delay, mistakes by Church people. How is it possible that the gospel does not work, that the Lord does not act, that this situation is not freed up? I have the impression that some who leave the priesthood because of a crisis of faith, do so because of this hidden gap between what the young priest in the seminary expected (the word of God fully effective, the Church filled with Christ's strength) and the reality of things: sadness, stagnation, frustration, tiredness, narrow mindedness, greed. How come there is all this, given what they promised us? Then faith in God, as it was conceived, fails.

They can also be more personal, simple things: the gap between my apostolic effort, what I do for the apostolate, and the disappointing result I get. When this continues, after a while it creates a certain discomfort, uncertainty, discouragement, frustration. So am I out of order? Does God really want me here? So why does he not help me? If I am under obedience, why are things not going well for me? Has obedience gulled me? Why has God allowed this deception? The same goes for the apparent uselessness of prayer. For someone who really prays we know how terrible the trials of prayer can be. They can be formidable tests of faith, the most fearful kind as described by those who have experienced them. And in general, everything that denotes lack of meaning, lack of significance of what we do can be included here. This lack of meaning produces a more psychic depression that also makes us doubt the ultimate foundation which gives meaning to everything, God's promise.

Here then are some examples of these tests. Each of you can multiply them according to experience. Thanks be to God our many trials, never lacking, are generally a test of the cardinal virtues: prudence, justice, fortitude, temperance and these involve us in being strong, mortified, prudent, honest, courageous. They do not touch the foundation but there can be situations which do, more or less.

3. Concluding reflections

I will offer some very simple reflections on these tests, starting with Abraham's test, as concluding suggestions.

Everyday tests

The first reflection is this: What do we find in the story of Abraham if we take it to be a typical story of the believer? We have to say that God tests us, that there are tests ahead, and as Sirach (Ecclesiasticus) Chapter 2 puts it well, picking up on elements found elsewhere in the Scriptures: 'My child, when you come to serve the Lord, prepare yourself for testing. Set your heart right and be steadfast, and do not be impetuous in time of calamity. Stay with the Lord. Cling to him and do not depart be prosperous...' (vv. 1-3). It is a very beautiful chapter: fear of God when we are being tested. So, tests exist and await us.

Why do they await us? What mysterious need requires them? Clearly, since the world is under the mark of the Evil one, meaning mankind is in an historical state of deterioration, it is inevitable for those who set about doing good that there will be obstacles. Our justice, fortitude, temperance are tested. It is difficult to be just, chaste, temperate, honest in a world which tends to be the opposite, hence it is absolutely inevitable in life that we will be tested.

However, one could say something more: why be tested? And why in particular be tested to the extreme or at least in that direction? I can offer an answer but I don't know if it is fully correct: because God is God. He gives himself in faith, through a journey of faith, and this journey of faith presumes we go beyond a largely mistaken original notion of God, at least in part, therefore one to be corrected, and as a consequence this implies a series of crises in our idea of God and of our identity before God. This is a terrible fundamental test. There is a basic reason: God is the God of promise, salvation, free initiative, of the word. We, instead, instinctively want a God of security with clear and evident foundations, a God we know everything about, whom we can foresee so that we can plan our way. The clash between these two things is the test. The test is understanding that God is different from how we had understood him. In fact, often the implicit reasoning in the test is this: Why does God not help me? Either I have not understood him or he doesn't exist! Here is the test, between these two.

Tests are there and they await us. Again I would say: the fact of being tested is the test, and we can fail. This is why the test is a risk for us. We can fail and people do, including where faith is concerned. Every day we can fail in faith. As St Paul says, certain people (he was talking about Alexander) have suffered shipwreck in the faith. We can be shipwrecked in faith, whatever situation we are in, even as Pope. St Ignatius puts it well, the devil spares no state or condition of person; no one is spared – everyone is to be tested. Indeed I would say that the more a person is involved in the things of God the more they are tempted regarding their image of God, because they have greater need to purify this image until the cedars of Lebanon fall – so what will become of us who are not the cedars of Lebanon?

The absurdity of certain exceptional tests

Second reflection: tests as such, just because they are a test, have something of the incomprehensible and the absurd about them. This is the drama of the test. While being tested in the area of the cardinal virtues is usually something we can perceive rationally – for example, I feel a strong sexual attraction: a test I can use my reason to understand that it is not good, so I fight it, make an effort, or in other words deal with it in a rational framework. On the contrary, the test we are talking about has aspects of incomprehensibility, absurdity as was the case for Abraham, because it is something that almost seems to go beyond the limits. It is difficult to express this but it seems, at least to me, that it says something, especially if we interpret it in terms of the supreme test, death. Death is the complete opposite to God's promise of life. Death shows degradation, decadence, the complete opposite of what God has promised us; it is the test with more of the incomprehensible and absurd about it. And that makes it a risk, because when we have understood it the test is over.

When the test is only a test

This leads to the third reflection: if this is the test, what is the gospel, the kerygma we can apply to it as drawn from the story of Abraham and interpreted from the scriptures as a whole?

Someone might think, and we often do so, that we are talking about a consoling kerygma. St Ignatius too, in his eighth rule for the discernment of spirits [321] says: 'When one is in desolation, he should consider that consolation will soon return.' Thus it is when we say to someone who is being tested: Courage, others have been tested like this, it will pass!

Instead, others insist on what we might call the 'heroic' kerygma – the moment for being courageous and showing what we are made of. St Ignatius records this in the ninth rule [322]: 'God wishes to try us, to see how much we are worth and how much we will advance in his service and praise when left without the generous reward of consolations and signal favours.' He wants to show us how capable we are of doing things both when left to our natural strengths and with his grace, which is always there even if we do not feel it.

While these two kerygmas are valid, in my opinion they take their validity from another, much deeper kerygma which is precisely Genesis 22:1: 'God tested Abraham,' meaning that the test is the test. Once someone has understood this, the test changes its meaning completely. We often hear it said; yes, I am in this state, but if I were to understand that it is a test, well then, I would be at peace, I could give meaning to what is happening to me. This is the fundamental gospel: the test is God's test and I am in his hands. Even in the depths of God's obscurity – to the point of saying like I think St Teresa of the Child Jesus said in the final months of her life, 'I have taken my place at the table of the unbelievers,' that is, she had reached her limit in the test of faith – in the greatest suffering faced with imminent death, you are in God's hands. Of its nature the test tends to have me say that God has abandoned me, that there is no God, but the gospel tells me: you are being tested, you are in God's hands. This brings it all back to the dynamics of the promise, and abandoning ourselves to the word.

This is what St Ignatius suggests in the seventh rule of discernment [320]: 'When one is in desolation, he should be mindful that God has left him to his natural powers to resist... He can resist with the help of God, which always remains.' We need to understand that it is God who is testing us, even if this is often very difficult to understand. We understand it for others but not so easily for ourselves. For ourselves it represents a problem we have been saddled with, a dramatic situation we cannot escape from, and then we lack all he energy to clarify matters.

We can further ask ourselves; Where does the gospel of Abraham's test go, where does it end? The answer is given us in the Letter to the Romans 8:31-32: 'If God is for us, who is against us? He who did not withhold his own Son, but gave him up for all of us, will he not with him also give us everything else?' Which is to be read in immediate parallel with Genesis 22:12: 'Now I know that you fear God, since you have not withheld your son, your only son, from me.'

The New Testament tradition has read God's love in Abraham's story. By giving us his Son he assures us that no test of any kind can ever go beyond what it is – a test; it cannot separate us from God's love. For God's part the test remains that and will not become a scandal:

> Who will separate us from the
> love of Christ? Will hardship,
> or distress, or persecution, or famine,
> or nakedness, or peril, or sword?
> As it is written, 'For your sake we
> are being killed all day long;
> we are accounted as sheep to be
> slaughtered.' No, in all these things
> we are more than conquerors through
> him who loved us. For I am
> convinced that neither death, nor life,

> nor angels, nor rulers, nor things
> present, nor things to come, nor
> powers, nor height, nor depth,
> nor anything else in all creation,
> will be able to separate us from
> the love of God in Christ Jesus our
> Lord (Rom 8:35-39).

The test is the test from a God who holds us firmly in his hand.

Eighth Meditation
Jesus' tests

In this meditation we enter into the spirit of the Third Week which, according to St Ignatius, results in compassion with Christ: feeling sorrow with the sorrowful Christ, suffering with the suffering Christ, entering into the mystery of his passion. This is about a contemplative grace, at least in the broad sense, and one that touches closely on the person in that it involves the inner being rather than the purely rational faculties. It is a grace that it is not possible to explain nor establish as a goal except from a distance. There is a risk of just mouthing words without managing to cross the threshold of real contact with the mystery.

After having contemplated the story of Abraham, our father in faith, we will contemplate some scenes in the life of Christ, head and completion of our faith – *archegòs kai teleiotés tes pìsteos*. I will offer three contemplations: Luke 4, Jesus in the desert; Luke 22, Jesus in the Garden of Gethsemane; Luke 23, Jesus on the cross. Along with this I will suggest why it seems to me that there is a contemplative link between these three scenes. Clearly, this link is of a logical nature. It then depends on the grace of prayer to move to contemplation which stirs the emotions and that cannot be expressed in words.

Three instances of temptation

Why have I chosen these texts? I have chosen them because they are in some way connected with temptation – *peirasmòs* – and with being tested. In the first instance, this is explicit because it says that Jesus was led by the Spirit into the desert for forty days, where he was tempted by the devil. The passage dealing with the Garden, the Mount of Olives, is also expressly presented under the label of temptation, at least as it was considered by Jesus' disciples. In fact, Luke 22:40 says: 'When he reached the place, he said to them, "Pray that you might not come into the time of trial."' And again at v. 46: "Get up and pray that you might not come into the time of trial." So temptation is near, imminent. We are in the same context, so, by analogy we can reflect on Jesus' situation in the Garden of Gethsemane as one of trial, merging with it as if we were there.

The third scene, the insults hurled from beneath the cross, is not of itself explicitly presented as temptation, but it seems to me that in the light of the other two, it has this character, both in the literary form it is presented in, but especially for the content. I refer to Luke 23:35 ff., when Jesus is crucified:

> And the people stood by, watching;
> but the leaders scoffed at him,
> saying, 'He saved others; let him
> save himself if he is the Messiah
> of God, his chosen one!' The
> soldiers also mocked him, coming

up and offering him sour wine
and saying, 'If you are the King
of the Jews, save yourself!'
There was also an inscription over
him, 'This is the King of the Jews.'
One of the criminals who were
hanged there kept deriding him
and saying, 'Are you not the
Messiah? Save yourself and us!'

Now these three scenes have been presented, we will put some questions to ourselves. The first is this: Who are the tempters in the three situations? The second: What is the formal literary structure and the object of the temptation in the individual cases? The third question: Where does the victory over the temptation lie in these three cases? Finally, a moment of reflection for us: What is involved for Jesus in the desert, on the cross, in the Garden of Gethsemane, and what is involved for us in similar situations in our lives?

1. Who are the tempters in the desert? The garden?

First question: Who are the tempters? According to Luke 4:3 it is the devil, *diabolus*, meaning the separator or the calumniator, the one who continuously tries to divide the unity of God's work, separate the human being from God by calumniating God in front of the human being, dividing one person from the others by calumniating the others: the others are taking you for a ride, they are attacking you; defend yourself, don't trust them. The devil also divides the human being internally: don't trust yourself. Pessimism.

This is the disintegrating activity opposed to God's unifying power. God unifies: the people, many together, interior life. The opposite is not to hope, not to unite, not to trust, not even oneself, which is despair: there is no salvation, no word of God, no meaning in things, no meaning in life! This comes out in various ways as real desperation, or an elegant kind of stoicism, or bitter resignation. Desperation becomes a kind of self-conceit, has its own philosophy, makes itself the *raison d'être* for this bitterness, this lack of meaning of things. Hence, it is the separator at work in the first scene.

Who is at work in the second scene? In Luke's text it says: 'Pray that you might not come in to the time of trial.' It presumes that temptation is present, imminent and there is a need to react strongly against it. In Matthew 26:38 something more is said: 'I am deeply grieved even to death; remain here and stay awake with me.' Here the tempter is sadness, heaviness. Then again at v. 41: 'Stay awake and pray, that you may not come into the time of trial. The spirit indeed is willing, but the flesh is weak.' Here the heaviness of the flesh is highlighted. It is not easy to interpret these words of Jesus. I would not see this as the Pauline 'spirit–flesh' opposition but the flesh understood as the human being deprived of the hope of grace, who falls when totally self-reliant. I would understand it in the Johannine sense of the Word made flesh, that is, human fragility: the spirit is willing but human beings sense their fragility. Jesus, too, felt this fragility, sadness, tedium, disgust which in itself has nothing negative about it. These things are the oppressiveness of the flesh. It is the human being faced with burdens that are heavier than can be managed, it seems. This is the tempter in the second scene.

Who are the tempters beneath the cross?

Who are the tempters in the third scene? Both Luke and John say it clearly. According to Luke it is the leaders who jeer while the people stand around looking on; then the soldiers and finally one of the malefactors crucified with Jesus.

Matthew 27:39 says: 'Those who passed by derided him, shaking their heads and saying, "*You who would destroy the temple and build it in three days, save yourself.*"' Then he adds: 'the chief priests also along with the scribes and elders, were mocking him, saying, "*He saved others, he cannot save himself.*"' There is a great variety of tempters: people passing by, bystanders representing vulgar, facile public opinion which is more easily influenced: Who is he? What has he done? Who did he think he was? Or the people as a whole. Luke spares these, almost wanting to say that deep down they respected, loved Jesus. And then the leaders, the people in charge, the high priests, scribes and elders, the religious men appointed to take care of the true image and worship of God; the intellectuals destined to clarify, refine and authentically present the word of God; the depositories of Israel's wisdom, the understanding Israel believed it had achieved of the God of Abraham, Isaac and Jacob. Also the soldiers, the forces of law and order, the executors, those who promote and sustain the leaders' world view. Finally a thief, one of the desperate ones, the socially excluded types who have lost any awareness of the meaning of life and empty their desperation out onto someone whose actions they do not understand.

It is a very broad scenario of the world of temptation. We come into it, too, to some extent, that is, as the intellectuals, religious men, holders of a right understanding of God. This relationship of class can only be disturbing for us, since it links us with some of those who were insulting Jesus at the foot of the cross.

2. What is the formal structure of the temptations?

The second question. Let us try to closely examine the formal structure and object of the temptations.

In the temptations in the desert, the structure of the first of them employs somewhat generic terms in the conditional: if you are this, then do such and such. It begins from a certain hypothesis which is the current image of God and draws consequences from it: if you are the Son of God... We all know what it means to be the Son of God: holder of power, judgement, the kingdom with all the privileges that go with it. So do this, or in other words carry out works of power. It is a similar temptation on the cross, also in the conditional, with hypotheses that represent 'common opinion', the opinion of the people passing by beneath the cross; the opinion of the leaders, high priests, elders, and also of the soldiers and the unfortunate man crucified with Jesus: if you are a great man, then do what a great man does, show us who you are.

The second temptation in the desert, which is the central one in Luke, is more disconcerting. It, too, is in the conditional but in a slightly different form, in the hypothesis: 'To you I will give their glory and all this authority; for it has been given over to me and I will give it to anyone I please. If you, then, will worship me, it will all be yours.' Here the hypothesis starts out from a fundamental datum: it is all mine. If you worship me it is all yours. This is the conceit many people have, that the key to history is in the hands of the shrewd, the ones with power, and if this is so it is better to be allied with them. It is the temptation to line up behind those who appear to hold all the important cards in history, including the ones that work for good ends. If you are my ally we will do, you will do great things. You can have great renown; your message will be heard. What is at play here is a certain way of acting in the world when we ally ourselves with those who have power of any kind.

What is the object of the temptations?

That is the structure. What is the object of the temptations?

In the first case we are dealing precisely with a certain concept of divine activity, of divine prerogatives and prestige: if you are the Son of God, even if not in a strictly theological, trinitarian sense; if you are the friend, the beloved of God, then the privilege of God is this, and everyone expects that you will act out of this privilege. If you truly want to obtain something, take account of the powers that operate, know how to look to those who can help you and can prevent you from being suppressed by human conflict.

The object of the first temptation is also a certain way of being Messiah, which in turn implies a certain image of the God who sends this Messiah. How can you represent God, the great, the powerful, *el Shaddai*, he who makes the mountains leap like goats and brings down the cedars of Lebanon, if you do not do some works of power? What is at stake here is the way Jesus must present the concept of God, his prerogatives, his perspective.

What is the object of the temptation in the Garden of Gethsemane? Clearly, it is very different from the previous one, but just the same I can see a similarity, some analogy. We can examine Jesus' prayer which is also in the conditional. In Luke: 'if you are willing'; in Matthew: 'if it is possible, let this cup pass from me.' What does it mean: if you are willing, if it is possible? It means: if it is part of your plan of salvation I would like, O God, not to have to drink this bitter cup.

In the desert, it was the case of the prestige of the Son of God; here, it is the case of the same Son's human weakness. There is a direct link between the choice he makes in the desert not to use his prestige as Son, and the choice in the Garden which necessarily leads to submitting to the consequences of weakness. While in the desert, he could have chosen to turn stones into bread. In the Garden, feeling grieved even to death, he could have employed means to escape this sadness. Instead, by saying, 'I am grieving even to death,' I cannot stand this, my weakness has reached its limits, I am at the limit of my psychological and physical strength, Jesus shows that he wants to experience this terrible moment so difficult to comprehend, a little like the cloud that covers Mount Moriah which it is not possible to fully penetrate.

In the Garden, Jesus makes the choice of weakness, just as he had made the choice of rejecting privileges in the desert. But he feels all the bitterness of the moment. God worked no miracle of giving him a happy Messiahship. Jesus chose the way of a humble Messiahship and must let the consequences come to the point of saying: I can't take any more.

The object of the temptation on the cross

The third temptation: Luke 23:35, 37, 39 on the cross. What is the object of this? The literary form is still in the conditional. The leaders say: if you are the Christ of God, if you are his chosen one, save yourself. The soldiers say: if you are the King of the Jews, save yourself. One of the criminals says: are you not the Christ? Save yourself and us too.

The object is once more the image of God as Saviour, but more theologically and in a more refined manner: if you are truly connected with God, if you speak so much of God as salvation, let us see him, show him to us and we will believe you. If you present yourself as the messianic king, the messianic king is the one who helps the poor, the miserable, prisoners, so let us see him. If you are really the awaited Messiah show us the messianic goods and we will believe you.

It seems to me that here Jesus truly arrives at the peak of his temptations, at the apex of the conflict of duties, which the Genesis text does not stress but in real terms is what moderns see in the episode involving Abraham. If he kills his son, Abraham sins gravely against his highest duty; if he does not kill him he sins against God. Here, he is caught in a trap he cannot escape from, at least in our modern mentality. The ethical order of things clearly tells him: do not touch the son, while the order of listening to the word seems to be telling him: kill him. Here is Abraham's drama and test, caught between one and the other.

We can imagine this drama of Abraham's in terms of our personal experience. Each of us, when reading it, feels involved in various ways. For Christ, the drama is clearer, inasmuch as it develops along the lines of the great theological terms of salvation: God the Messiah, messianic King, Saviour – all terms Jesus triggered in the minds of his listeners, and now expressed in dialectical form in the dilemma which is logically ridiculous but dramatic in its reality: if you come down from the cross they will believe you, they will say that the God of Israel has sent the Saviour.

A God who does not know how to save

Yet, what God will they believe in? They will believe in the God of power, the God who profits from his privileges, not in a God who does not spare his only Son, the God who makes himself weak. If he does not come down, they will not believe, so why so much suffering? Why death on the cross?

Here is the terrible climax of the situation Jesus finds himself in: the clash between two images of God. The common folk, public opinion, the leaders, scribes, intellectuals and elders say: we have this image of God and we will believe you if you bring it to realisation. Jesus, in the name of the image he represents, does not respond, does nothing, because if he were to do something he would deny his mission, would deny his image of God.

In his flesh, Jesus experiences the scandal of a God who does not know how to save. The thief says: save yourself if you are the Son of God, and save us. If you cannot, if you do not want to save yourself, at least save us, let us feel your power. The Gentiles, one Psalm says, are praying to a God who cannot save. In himself, Jesus experiences the terrible scandal of manifesting to the intelligentsia of Israel the image of a God like the pagan god who cannot save.

3. How does the victory come about?

The third question: How does the victory over temptation come about? I will very simply say: the victory does not come about through theological reasoning, a broad explanation, but on the basis of facts, reality, things seen, through obedience.

Jesus says: 'it is written', meaning we must obey the word of God. Do not get into debates about the concept of God, the concept Abraham, could have had in Ur of the Chaldeans, or one gradually purified through the promise. Yes, God showed his power to Abraham but he also showed him that this power does not scorn the weakness involved in the expectation of it, and demands abandonment to him to the extent to which the flaming torch of the promise of a son, Isaac, seems to be snuffed out. In this weakness too, God manifests himself. God is ready to strip himself of his privileges at a certain point.

The New Testament also uses this reasoning. Jesus replies to Satan by declaring his obedience to God: 'it is written' – man does not live by bread alone; you will serve and adore the Lord your God; you will not put the Lord your God to the test. In the Garden too, the victory is through obedience: let your will, O God, be done, your plan be fulfilled whatever it may be.

Jesus does not enter into debate, because these are things that cannot be explained in words, or explained when obedience has been proposed and accepted. Jesus does not even debate the matter with himself but throws himself in through obedience. Even on the cross he does not say a word about it. Paradoxically, he could have come down from the cross and said: now I can explain God's mysterious weakness to you, the true notion of God I am revealing to you. By doing that, Jesus would have contradicted God's weakness, hence he does nothing except stay where he is, accepting the opposition, the insults, lack of belief, rejection, and misunderstanding. The only thing he does is an act of love and friendship by reassuring the thief who trusted in him. According to the other evangelists, Jesus says nothing. However, Luke 23:46 records his last words: 'Father, into your hands I commend my spirit' – obedience to the very end.

The lesson for us: three levels of obedience

In contemplating this scene we could say: Lord Jesus, obedient unto death, grant us this victory in which the true face of God is shown in me, in others, through the Church.

We could perhaps use another word in place of obedience. For us, obedience comes from faith, while for Jesus it comes from abandonment and love. It seems to me that here we are touching closely on St Ignatius' three levels, three degrees of humility, or of obedience, submission, love, the most perfect of which comes to accept the image of God revealed by Christ stripped of his privilege out of love. The ultimate root of this, Jesus tells us in John, and in Paul's Letter to the Galatians: John 15:15 ff.: 'No one has greater love than this, to lay down one's life for one's friends... I have called you friends'; Galatians 2:20: '(He) loved me and gave himself for me.'

It is true, Abraham excels in faith. The word 'love' does not appear in his story, but his entire life is life as a friend. God considers him a friend, trusts him. In the New Testament love and faith are clearly linked, especially in Romans 5:1 which concludes the episode about Abraham (Chapter 4): 'Since we are justified by faith we have peace with God through our Lord Jesus Christ... because God's love has been poured into our hearts through the Holy Spirit that has been given to us.'

The theme of God's love in us is clarified by the theme of obedience, abandonment, dedication, in the theme of faith which is the victory that overcomes temptation, overcomes the world.

NINTH MEDITATION
Abraham's consolation and Christ the consoler

This meditation all turns on Genesis 23: Abraham's purchase of the Machpelah cave, the purchase of a burial site.

We have not yet done a 'composition of place', a '*videndo locum*' as St Ignatius says, or an appeal to the senses, the imagination assisted by memory to look at the place, as we could do here, at least for someone who has been there, considering the shrine at Hebron from up close or from a distance; the cave of the Patriarchs where the Muslim tradition jealously looks after the burial site of Abraham, Sarah, Isaac, Jacob, Rebecca. It does so with such ardent devotion that it goes to the extent of fanaticism in the struggle between the Arabs and the Jews, who also have a small synagogue there. This very evocative place, so fascinating and mysterious, which when seen from afar looks like a kind of rock cave perched on a mountainside. From our perspective, we could connect it with Christ's tomb in Jerusalem. We can look at these two things together, connect them. The grace we ask for will be to understand something of Abraham's consolation, to understand ultimately the power of Christ the consoler.

The meditation points are as follows: first a reading of and reflection on Genesis 23; second, just a brief reflection on Luke 24, the chapter where Jesus consoles the disciples from Emmaus, who in a way function as a point of reference for the story of Abraham's burial site.

1. Abraham's burial site

The title speaks of 'Abraham's consolation'. The book of Genesis does not describe Abraham's death at length, as perhaps would have been right for a Patriarch, and as does the apocryphal literature, especially when it narrates the death of the twelve Patriarchs one after the other, with a great abundance of details, testaments, recommendations to sons etc. Genesis is very sober in its description of Abraham's death. In Chapter 25:7-10 it says that 'the length of Abraham's life (was) one hundred and seventy-five years.'

> Abraham breathed his last and died
> in a good old age, an old man full
> of years, and was gathered to his
> people. His sons Isaac and Ishmael
> buried him in the cave of Machpelah
> in the field of Ephron, son of Zohar
> the Hittite, east of Mamre, the field
> that Abraham purchased from the Hittites.
> There Abraham was buried, with
> his wife Sarah.

As we see, here it is the burial site more than the death that is important – the purchase of the site from Ephron, close to Mamre etc. It seems that the Abraham story cycle gives a certain significance to this tomb. It becomes clear if we take the whole of Chapter 23, one of the most enjoyable, most beautiful of the episodes in the cycle, rich in popular folklore, fully dedicated to the purchase of the burial site. One could ask, why such an account in a story like Abraham's which focuses wholly on great fundamental issues: the call, God's promise, the response, or describing a business contrast between Orientals; the shrewdness, various maneouvers. Why? It is precisely here that we will take a brief but close look at things, firstly by reading Chapter 23 - tell the story faithfully, St Ignatius says - then by studying the passage in its structure and parts, then finally some reflection.

What is the importance of this passage? Why so much concern to describe the purchase of the burial site? The account begins with an introduction: Sarah's death and mourning for her. It then moves on to the negotiation for the site in four well-measured steps clearly distinct from one another. Sarah's death: 'Sarah lived one hundred twenty-seven years; this was the length of Sarah's life.' It is a Priestly account but makes use of an older document, as the Jerusalem Bible tells us: 'Sarah died at Kiriath-arba (that is, Hebron' - the ancient name of the city is recorded - 'in the land of Canaan' - note the painful mention: Canaan, a foreign land - 'and Abraham went in to mourn for Sarah and to weep for her.' Perhaps he was away pasturing his flock. The introduction tells us that Sarah dies in a foreign land. The promise did not come true for her. Then the negotiation begins, split into four parts, as I said. First the request, then the insistence, third the negotiation over the price and fourth and finally, the conclusion and agreement.

The request

The text says: 'Abraham rose up from beside his dead.' This is one of the few sentimental notes in the text. Abraham weeps, then at a certain point gets up. He has certain duties to perform so he leaves the mourning aside, 'and said to the Hittites…' (v. 3). Hittites is the generic name given to the local population. I don't think it bears any relation to the historical Hittites, traces of whom have been found in excavations in Turkey; it became a common name for various earlier historical waits.

Abraham's speech, seen within the framework of the promise, is certainly a sorrowful one: 'I am a stranger and an alien residing among you.' Abraham is in a foreign land. As the depository of the promise of land he can only say: I am a foreigner passing through among you, 'give me property among you for a burying place so that I may bury my dead out of sight.' This is a very humble request: give me the possibility of burying one of my own who has died. We have to presume that Abraham is living as a nomad but is on good terms with the local population. He had permission for his shepherding which he would ask as needed, and the population respected him, so social relationships were good. Nevertheless, Abraham was considered to be a stranger, and to carry out this important act of ownership, to bury a dead person in a precise visible spot which he could then recognise and venerate, there was need for the people to agree. The people understood that ownership had its beginning with this act, a handing over of certain legal rights and conditions to Abraham. So Abraham speaks, as we see from what follows, before the assembly at the gate to the city.

'The Hittites answered Abraham, "Hear us my lord; you are a mighty prince among us."' The style is elevated, as one would address a person being given great honour. Note the difference between what 'mighty prince' means for the people, a form of adulation for a man who has shown himself to be favoured by God, and what it means in the context of the promise. 'Bury your dead in the choicest of our burial places; none of us will withhold from you any burial ground for burying your dead.' The reply is obviously a negative one despite the effusion of courtesy, that is, all our burial sites are at your disposition for your dead but you do not have a site of your own. Yes, we like you, but you are still a guest, a foreigner.

The insistence

Now comes the insistence. The second step is presented like the others, by profound acts of humility on Abraham's part: 'Abraham rose and bowed to the Hittites...' We see this old man bowing, his head touching the ground, with everyone looking at him, then he gets up again. 'He said to them, "If you are willing that I should bury my dead out of my sight, hear me, and entreat for me Ephron son of Zoar so that he may give me the cave of Machpelah, which he owns; it is at the end of his field. For the full price let him give it to me in your presence as a possession for a burying place."' (vv. 7-9).

Abraham does not demur. He goes on the attack and indicates precisely what he wants, while earlier he had only spoken in general, even though he had something precise in mind, which emerges after his act of reverence and homage: I want that cave at the end of the field. He already has a clear plan he wishes to carry out. It makes an impression on Ephron who is surprised. He was not expecting this. He may have heard some rumours but pretends he knows nothing. The text says: 'Now Ephron was sitting among the Hittites; and Ephron the Hittite answered Abraham in the hearing of the Hittites of all who went in at the gate of his city...' The contract will be discussed at the city gate as a public act, before the assembly. '"No, my lord, hear me; I give you the field and I give you the cave that is in it; in the presence of my people I give it to you to bury your dead"' (vv 10-11). What has Abraham understood? He has understood that this is very special to him and he is giving it to him as a friend. Abraham is aware that the man wants to negotiate and will ask a very high price which will first need to be established.

Negotiations over price

And so we arrive at the negotiations over price. He could have said: with these conditions we will achieve nothing;

let's remain friends as before. I would rather give you my sheep. But Abraham really wants it. At all costs he wants to own the field and the cave, and feels an inner urge to have this piece of land. He once more introduces himself with an act of humility: 'Then Abraham bowed down before the people of the land. He said to Ephron in the hearing of the people of the land, "If you only will listen to me! I will give the price of the field; accept it from me so that I may bury my dead there."' Abraham begs him to accept the price and asks not to receive it as a gift. He wants to pay for it. Ephron replies: '"My Lord, listen to me; a piece of land worth four hundred shekels of silver – what is that between you and me? Bury your dead"' (vv. 12-15). It seems, at least according to what is said, that an enormously high price disappears; what are 400 silver shekels? I will gift you with the land.

What would Abraham have been able to do? The price seemed too high and certainly had to be a huge sacrifice for Abraham to pay. However, the text says: 'Abraham agreed with Ephron.' He so much wanted to arrive at the purchase that he no longer bargains, wants to take no more steps and accepts: 'Abraham weighed out for Ephron the silver that he had named in the hearing of the Hittites, four hundred shekels of silver, according to the weights current among the merchants' (v. 16).

Exegetes consider the final contract to be a true and proper act of land registration describing what is bought, how and where it is to be found and who the purchaser is: 'So the field of Ephron in Machpelah which was to the east of Mamre, the field with the cave that was in it and all the trees that were in the field, throughout its whole area, passed to Abraham as a possession in the presence of the Hittites, in the presence of all who went in at the gate of his city' (vv. 17-18). It was a contract which completely followed the rules, was official, and with all the precise indications of place: 'After this, Abraham buried Sarah his wife in the cave of the field of Machpelah facing Mamre (that is, Hebron) in the land of Canaan. The field and the cave that is in it passed from the Hittites into Abraham's possession as a burying place' (vv. 19-20). The text ends here by emphasising that finally this small plot of land in the land of Canaan belongs to Abraham.

It is sufficient for Abraham to have a small plot of land

Having explained the text, let us now do some reflection. The first reflection I would offer is this: Abraham needs very little to be satisfied. He has a son and he hopes that a people will issue from him. He has a son and very little of his own in the patriarchal sense of things. Not twelve sons like Jacob. Just one, a fragile hold on the promise, one who could die at any time. But he hopes for and sees the whole nation in this son, for in him is the pledge and sign of God's favour which he has fully, as know from Genesis 25:1 where he feels consoled after Sarah's burial:

> Abraham took another wife, whose name was Keturah. She bore him Zimran, Jokshan, Medan, Midian, Ishbak and Shuah. Jokshan was

> the father of Sheba and Dedan. The
> sons of Dedan were Asshurim,
> Letushim and Leummim. The sons
> of Midian were Ephah, Epher,
> Hanoch, Abida and Eldaah.
> All these were the children of Keturah (vv. 1-4).

So Abraham has his descendants!

Yet the text says: 'Abraham gave all he had to Isaac. But to the sons of his concubines Abraham gave gifts while he was still living, and he sent them away from his son Isaac, eastward to the east country' (vv. 5-6). Isaac was sufficient for Abraham. He could have put them together and made an alliance with Isaac as head of this federation. No. Isaac must remain alone as the son of the promise. God will provide for him. Isaac had been the reason for laughter (his name means cause of joy), at first ironical for Sarah but then cause for joyous laughter, the son of consolation. Just as an only son was enough for Abraham, as a sign and pledge, guarantee and anticipation of a people, so also was it enough for him to have a small plot of land as sign and pledge of the promise, already his in some way. God has given him a tiny possession:

Acts 7:4-6, Stephen's speech, says:

> After his (Abraham's) father died,
> God had him move from there to
> this country in which you are now
> living. He did not give him any
> of it as a heritage, not even a foot's
> length, but promised to give it to

> him as his possession and to his
> descendants after him, even though
> he had no child.

Abraham had passed through the land of the promise, but no centimetre of the land he had trodden was his, not even a footprint. But here he has a tiny possession in which his faith sees an anticipation of the land. Sarah dies in the land of Canaan but she is not buried there, but in land which by now belongs to Abraham, and Abraham's body, too, will be buried in his land. At least in anticipation, figuratively, he already possesses something, and for him this something is cause for huge consolation. For someone who believes, has gambled his entire existence on the word of God, even a small sign, an anticipation which might seem very little to others, is an immense joy, because this little is the guarantee of God's love which promises everything.

The guarantee: the Spirit in our hearts

Here I mention some New Testament texts which continue, specify, illuminate this economy of God's with Abraham and ourselves.

In 2 Corinthians 1:20-22 it says that all God's promises have become a 'yes' in Christ. God keeps his promises and 'has anointed us, by putting his seal on us and giving us his Spirit in our hearts as a first instalment.' What is the first instalment, this guarantee of the Spirit? It is little compared to the expected fullness, but it is already everything, already the anticipated fullness of the promised gift.

The same thought, in different words, is expressed in Romans 5:5. 'Hope does not disappoint us, because God's love has been poured into our hearts through the Holy Spirit that has been given to us.' And again in Romans 8:11: 'If the Spirit of him who raised Jesus from the dead dwells in you, he who raised Christ from the dead will give life to your mortal bodies also through his Spirit that dwells in you.' And finally, in the Letter to the Colossians 1:27: You are already dwelling with Christ in God, 'which is Christ in you, the hope of glory.' So, even if you apparently have very little, you have everything. People say: But what is a Christian? What do you rejoice over? What do you have that is different? Apparently very little, however, in reality you have the pledge of the complete promise, you have everything, which is the gift of Christ anticipated and the presence of the spirit.

So what is this first reflection telling us? It tells us to also let ourselves be consoled by the signs, the anticipations, the pledges of the promise! It is true, we must look to the fullness of the promise, but we must also look at the joy of the present, at all the pointers which already give us the certainty in the present that God's love is poured into our hearts.

Being buried in Christ

I would like to add a second reflection: the sign given to Abraham is not just a field but especially a burial place. It insists on the cave, the tomb. In the Abraham cycle the tomb as such does not have any deep theological significance. In fact, commentators rightly say that the tomb had no special significance for the Jews. There was no cult of the dead and indeed the cult of the dead was strongly criticised.

But it seems to me that to be buried, to have the burial site on a piece of the promised land, leads us to look at our being buried in Christ. Christ is the place, the promised land in which we were buried through baptism as Romans 6:4 reminds us: 'Therefore we have been buried with him by baptism into death, so that, just as Christ was raised from the dead by the glory of the Father, so we too might walk in newness of life.' Christ is our promised land and we have been inserted into him. From this, certainly in embryonic form, I suggest that after meditating on Abraham's burial site, we move on to meditate on Christ's, the place where the fullness of consolation is proclaimed, he who represents that fullness.

2. Christ our consoler

Second point for meditation: Christ the consoler. We can develop this point by comparing Christ the consoler with Abraham's small consolation which was already considerable for him. Where and how is Christ our consoler? As we read in Luke 24, Jesus is a consoler first through signs: the empty tomb, especially the stone rolled back, the angel's kerygma: he is not here, he is risen, he lives – all consoling signs that Jesus sends ahead of himself. But Jesus is not satisfied only with signs, not just with promises. The promises are not sufficient to bread the rock of incredulity, diffidence, fear. By contrast with Abraham who is content with signs, Jesus makes himself a consoler in friendly encounters. All the resurrection accounts speak of them, and St Ignatius proposes meditations on these in the Fourth Week.

How does Jesus console in these friendly encounters? We see it in his encounter with the Emmaus disciples: revealing himself gradually, starting with their sadness, their scepticism, the sense of defeat they have by now come to, even to the extent that the best news says nothing more to them. Yes, some women saw him, the Apostles have seen him, but it is all submerged in a sea of destructive scepticism. This is the situation Jesus begins from and gradually through his presence he consoles them, finally manifesting himself to them in the breaking of the bread. He himself, Jesus, is the kerygma, the promise to Abraham accomplished. He is the good news as Paul says: 'For in him every one of God's promises is a "yes"' (2 Cor 1:20).

Looking at Christ the consoler as he gradually draws closer to the Emmaus disciples, brings about a change of mood in them and warms their heart. We can make a negative comparison with Abraham. Recall that we said there are no consoling words or prophetic words of Abraham's recorded except for the slightest hint to Isaac in Genesis 22:8: 'God himself will provide… my son.' Abraham is a loner. He obeys God's command but he is not a man capable of helping others, creating community; he expects everything from God. He is not a consoler.

Jesus, instead, is quite the opposite. He is no loner and by nature is a consoler, loves being with others, goes looking for people, comes up from behind the disciples going to Emmaus, reaches them on their journey, creates new enthusiasm in them, and sees that they, too, run off to give the news, look for others. Jesus creates community. Abraham is content with being faithful to the word, keeping it in his heart, convincing others within the family circle as much as he can, for example Sarah, but without great success. Sarah laughs at God's promise. Jesus spreads consolation, communion, trust around him, and from a group of people lacking confidence he soon re-establishes men full of joy, peace, who rejoice in his presence, receive his words and with his Spirit then carry his name and in turn become consolers.

Here we could reconsider Paul's exclamation in 1 Corinthians 13:13: faith and hope are great 'but the greatest of these is love.' Abraham's faith is great, huge, but greater still is Christ's love. He succeeds in forming a community, starting with men lacking confidence. He gives them drive, enthusiasm, a sense of God's fullness.

3. The 'principle and foundation' of Abraham's story

I have also thought of a third point, a kind of last word on all the Abraham story. I asked myself: What is the principle and foundation of the story of Abraham? In looking for it I seemed to find it in Genesis 12:1 initially: 'God said to Abraham,' God's word which marks a new beginning, like a new creation in Abraham's life. However, I then thought that this word of God should have an introduction, an ultimate principle and foundation, and I think I have found it in the light of St Ignatius' last meditation, the 'Contemplation to attain the love of God' especially in the fourth point where it says: 'This is to consider all blessings and gifts as descending from above. Thus my limited power comes from the supreme and infinite power above' [237]. This supreme and infinite power is what St Ignatius speaks of at the beginning of the *Exercises*: '*Homo creatus est*' [23]. Man is created... So, using the words of Scripture we can more clearly express the principle and foundation of Abraham's story with Genesis 14:22 – a slightly isolated verse that could seem to be a message preceding the story itself – where Abraham, speaking with the king of Sodom, rejects the booty and says: 'I have sworn to the LORD, God Most High, maker of heaven and earth.' God the creator of heaven and earth, God the creator of man, namely, Genesis 1, it seems, is the principle and foundation which the Priestly and Yahwist sources have put as a premise to the story of Abraham. We are invited, I think, in retrospect, to seek the principle and foundation of all this story and the history of salvation in the absolute fullness of God, the God of glory, creator of all things.

I am urged to consider this by Acts 7:2 which begins the story of Abraham with a sentence that is not at the beginning of the story in Genesis 12: 'Brothers and fathers listen to me. The God of glory appeared to our ancestor Abraham.' So Abraham's story opens with the God of power whose glory was first manifested in all of creation. I am also urged on by Romans 4:17, where there is a comparison between the power of the resurrection in which Abraham believed, and God's creative power: Abraham our father 'in the presence of the God in whom he believed, who gives life to the dead and calls into existence the things that do not exist.' The God who calls into existence the things that do not yet exist, who gives life to the dead, is the principle and foundation of Abraham's journey of faith.

What do I mean by retrospectively seeing God the Creator as the beginning of the whole Abraham story? I want to say that God, as Creator, especially of mankind, the human person, so, insofar as he is not extraneous to us, is the ultimate and immediate foundation of my personal existence; the one whose good and loving will make me who I am, a person called by him by name. This God, by virtue of this primordial intimacy, can call me his son, giving me the promise that is realised in his Son or, if we want to use St Ignatius' words: 'putting me with the son.' Contemplation of this promise of God in Christ allows us to understand how the story of Abraham is the story of God's work in me, the God who puts me with his Son who is the root of who I am. In this root of who I am I receive a new creating word of God's love, placing me within his own divine life.

Why God is all in all

We also have a point of reference for this primordial permanence in 1 Corinthians 15:28, where it mysteriously describes the end of everything with the sentence: *o Theòs to pānta en pâsin* – God all in all. What does it mean? That when everything will be subjected to God, the text says, also he, the Son, 'will also be subjected to the one who put all things in subjection under him, so that God may be all in all.' Hence the end of everything, all mysteriously taken up in the Father. It is a perspective in which, it seems to me, it is possible to understand St Ignatius' strange conclusion, which invites us into the fourth point of the *'contemplatio ad amorem'* to consider everything in God, all as coming from God.

I asked myself, but could not reply: How come St Ignatius, who began from such a clear concept of creation (man is created, divine transcendence, man's obedience), arrives in this fourth point at a description of an almost emanative kind, of things coming from God: justice, goodness, piety, mercy all descend from the supreme and infinite power, just as rays of light descend from the sun, and as waters flow from their fountains? We know that theologically, this perspective is very risky and could lead to a pantheistic concept. But it seems to me that in his simplicity, after having started out from God's absolute transcendence, St Ignatius had seen that God's love and our 'being put' with Christ is revealed in this transcendence. He sees everything in a divine light and really, without any risk he recognises all things as rays reflecting this infinite power. He especially recognises our personal existence as grace, as the promise realised in us by Christ, not as something that places us at a distance or in simple obedience, but as indescribable communion with the God of the promise.

It seems to me that this third point could set in motion a certain *'contemplatio ad amorem'* which takes account of what Abraham's and Christ's experience have led us to grasp of our understanding of God.

PART TWO
INSTRUCTIONS

First Instruction
The dynamics of God's word

This instruction on the dynamics of God's word is inspired, even though by analogy, by St Ignatius' *Spiritual Exercises*, in the second meditation of the first Week, the one on sins which the Saint calls the '*processus peccatorum*' or listing of sins [56]. In our case we will be looking back over our own lives with Abraham in mind, not looking back in a specifically moral way, that of the first or third fruits of the twentieth introductory observation, nor even in the particularly ascetic way of making the better choice. Instead, we will look back over our religious experience, our way of living the reality of God in its essence – a religious experience with all that this involves, the light, the shade, presence and absence.

With this in mind, I think we can substantially apply the structure of the Ignatian meditation [55-61] to this experience, especially the *exclamatio admirativa* or cry of wonder [60] clearly applied to Abraham. If Abraham, having come to the end of his life, had to say what he had understood after so many religious experiences, his cry of wonder, in my view, would be Saint Augustine's '*Quam sero te cognovi!*' How late have I come to know thee! Or in other words, the more I thought I knew you the less I actually know you! I think perhaps this cry would be the result of all our meditations. How little I know God in reality! The more I thought I knew him, the less, I now acknowledge, I really did know him. In a certain sense, God becomes more mysterious, more beyond our grasp.

The dynamics of God's word

I will briefly sum up a second Ignatian note I would like to draw your attention to: it is the dynamics of God's word in the *Exercises*, beginning with two biblical texts, Luke 8 on 'the seed is the word' and the other famous one from Isaiah 55:10 ff., where the word of God carries out its action: 'as the rain and snow come down from heaven and do not return there until they have watered the earth, making it bring forth and sprout, giving seed to the sower and bread to the eater, so shall my word be that goes out from my mouth; it shall accomplish that which I purpose, and succeed in the thing for which I sent it.' That is, God's word runs the course of this dynamic parabola: it goes out, comes down, goes to work, then returns.

Starting out from these two texts, I propose to sum up some typical points of the dynamic of the word in the *Exercises*.

It is not enough for God's word to be heard, meditated upon, contemplated in meditation or contemplation. It needs to germinate in the colloquy of prayer. The colloquy of prayer then needs to extend to the colloquy of resonance which is contact with the retreat director or in group reflection. The colloquy of prayer and resonance is offered at some point after the meditation on the Kingdom. It becomes an invitation to choice, decision, an audit of our life, then we need to go back to the word in the process of real life.

What is the extreme importance of this dynamic process of the word which St Ignatius also proposes in the *Spiritual Exercises* and which is analogous to Isaiah 55 and Luke 8? The word of God, which is a small seed, hence something very fragile, suffocates and dies if it is not developed. It is futile to throw it down endlessly, always staying with the first instance of contemplative meditation, if it does not break through into prayer, prayer which is communicated, shared and leads to choices, decisions etc.

It is in this dynamic that God can be recognised as 'God', that is as holy. God's word can be known as God's word only when it is allowed to run its course in us. Otherwise it is smothered, and our understanding of God then becomes an objectifying, generic one, all those aberrant forms of religiosity we will briefly talk about again with biblical reference.

A threefold law

I will add one further note: these seven points I have mentioned in the dynamics of the word (they could lead to others such as confession, penance etc.) – meditation-contemplation, colloquy of prayer, colloquy of resonance, offer, choice, decision, audit – are things we should all do. A threefold law applies to these seven points which I will call the law of balance, rhythm, measure.

– The law of balance means that these seven points have to be in balance, it is possible for there to be an abnormal development of religious experience if everything becomes choice and decision without contemplation, hearing the word without resonance: or if everything is resonance without choice and checking on decisions made. In other words, these elements have a balance which needs to be preserved. When it is not preserved, our experience of God suffers, our religious experience suffers.

– As well as rhythm, all this also need measure. Measure means we can exaggerate our resonance as happens in groups where they only talk, talk about God's word, which in the end comes to nothing because it is constantly being spoken of. Or there can be a lack of measure by focusing entirely on verification, verifying what we are doing, have done. All the focus is on lack of sufficiency.

Or there is a lack of measure if everything is focused intellectually on contemplation of the word, analysing the text. Contextualising, looking at structure. In the end it smothers the word. In a way, the word kills itself, it dies.

So lack of balance, rhythm and measure alternate and hinder the process of the word and close off our understanding of God. In the end we reach a point of practical atheism. We admit of God because we have to, but he has no more practical resonance in our life, just because this process of the word, this circulation of the word has not taken place, has been blocked.

We could mention another important New Testament text on the dynamic of the word in the *Exercises*. The text is Colossians 3:16 ff: 'Let the word of Christ dwell in you richly; teach and admonish one another in all wisdom; and with gratitude in your hearts sing psalms, hymns and spiritual songs to God. And whatever you do, in word or deed, do everything in the name of the Lord Jesus, giving thanks to God the Father through him.' Here, too, we see the magnificent path taken by the word: the word comes, dwells, resounds, is sung, repeated, taught by one another, expressed in songs and works, and it all resounds to the glory of God the Father. Here is the experience of God through the process of the word and its dynamic.

I would like to make a third observation starting from the *Exercises*, that is, an extension of the daily meditation to two biblical texts I found in the readings for Saturday of the 12th Week of the Year, which made a great impression on me.

Victims of religious alienation

One is Colossians 1:21 which I suggest as a further exploration of the theme: where Abraham started out from, where we have come from, where the person to whom is offered the grace of a gospel understanding of God has come from. Paul says: 'And you who were once estranged and hostile in mind, doing evil deeds.' This text impressed me a lot, especially in the Greek version due to the words it uses: Who were you? Who was Abraham before he came to know God? Who was the human being before coming to a true gospel understanding of God? The Greek says he was an *apellotriomenos*, someone alienated, experiencing profound religious alienation. He thinks he knows God but does not know him: he is split in his understanding of God between the truth he understands and the things that disturb him, resulting in him not understanding.

This *apellotriomenos* is translated as 'estranged' but it really means a victim of religious alienation and represents precisely Abraham's point of departure in his search for God.

Rightly at this point the Jerusalem Bible says that 'estranged' (*abalienati* in the Vulgate) is in reference to God, not Israel, and in this regard quotes a parallel passage from Ephesians 4:18, also very important, because it more or less refers to the starting point, the *'unde'*, the 'from whence': 'You must no longer live as the Gentiles live, in the futility of their minds. They are darkened in their understanding, alienated from the life of God.' These are very strong words In the Greek, the word corresponding to 'darkened', *eskotomenoi*, means full of blind spots in their understanding of God, full of alienation, ignorance of God, deviation. The Gentile understanding is described as darkened, alienated, obscuring, deviant. This is rough language if we consider that the pagans, the Gentiles, were very religious, people who called on God all day long, lived a continually active life of sacrifice, favours supplication, prayers. This description of the deviant tendency of our efforts at seeking God, the way Paul presents it to us, seems to me to be important.

A *threat for us Christians too*

We could say this is about pagans, not about us. But to me it seems to be about anyone who seeks to know God, starting from a position of alienation, sin, darkness which is the historical world apart from God.

This is the situation we so often start out from even if as St Paul puts it well in Colossians 1:22, things have changed. 'He has now reconciled (us)... Provided that you continue securely established and steadfast in the faith, without shifting from the hope promised by the gospel that you heard.' What does this text mean? It means that if the gospel is not always before us in its clarity, we return to our previous state. This state of religious alienation is a constant threat, this threat of blindness, obscurity, dark patches in our understanding of God. Every time we distance ourselves from the clear focus and well-measured flame of the gospel light, we fall back into a monistic, pharisaical religiosity which clings to forms and seeks to photocopy authentic religiosity by basing itself on external situations and traditions. This is so often our practical story.

It seems to me that what we can draw from these texts is that any religiosity, including a Christian one, when left to its own devices, is subject to a certain drag, a kind of entropy which worships a law or forms, and at a certain point can result in obfuscating our true understanding of God, even if it keeps the name, the worship, the ceremonies. I think it is a useful reality to consider in the setting of the First Week, reflecting not so much on the morality or immorality of this state, but on how real it is. It is not blameworthy but a real state of difficulty we actually experience in our understanding of God. It is Abraham's difficult journey.

Looking for Jesus' religiosity

To the two texts (Eph 4:18 and Col 1:21-23) we can add the Gospel text, Luke 6:1-5: Jesus rebukes the Pharisees' lack of religious freedom when they criticise the disciples for plucking heads of grain on the Sabbath. Clearly, here the two understandings are opposed: the understanding Jesus has of God, which is freeing in religious terms, and the Pharisaic understanding which in God's name sets itself in opposition to the understanding Jesus has of God. Here we clearly have the departure and arrival point: Abraham's astral religiosity, the religiosity based on forms, and Jesus' religiosity.

Tomorrow morning, we will meditate some more on this theme, shifting from the religious level to the moral one. We will try to see in what way a certain unclear understanding of God is reflected in ambiguous behaviour. We will attempt to take a better look at this in the example of Abraham.

Second Instruction
Reform of life, prolonged prayer, penitential spirit and community life

Before tackling this topic I want to say something about the *reformatio vitae*, reforming our life, in relation to the meditation on the Two Standards.

Conquest of self and regulation of one's life

I asked myself if it is possible to establish the place for the meditation on the Two Standards, bearing in mind the purpose of the *Exercises* as I have proposed them in the context of our reflections on Abraham. I remind you that I have sought to analyse the purposes of the *Exercises* from the title, namely; '*ut vincat seipsum homo*' or conquest of self; '*ordinet vitam suam*', or regulation of one's life; '*quin se determinet*'; in such a way that no decision is made under the influence of any inordinate attachment (21).

We have seen three stages in this purpose of the *Exercises* and a diversity of levels in these three stages: by managing to unmask and neutralise inordinate attachments it is possible to make a correct choice in regulating our life, which results in the victory of faith. On the other hand, the victory of faith – which chronologically speaking is not the last stage but actually the departure point – allows us to unmask inordinate attachments and see what true regulation of our life is, from which the victory of faith draws new light.

If this attempt to structure the title of the *Exercises* has some value, it seems to me that I should reply to the question of where to locate the meditation on the Two Standards: it is located at every crucial point in the *Exercises* when we try to draw some fruit from some of the meditations, those for example on the life of Jesus in view of a possible choice. In other words, in my opinion this meditation responds to the question: Which are the more devious impediments, the practical impediments in daily life, the 'chains and nets' that lie in wait to ambush me? The answer it gives is as follows: the trickiest traps, precisely because they are not hidden dangers as in the First Week, that is, breaking the commandments, openly doing wrong, are: possessiveness, pride, power, having more, being more, having more power. Every form and state of life, any situation people find themselves in, excluding no one, incurs these kinds of traps.

Dealing with inordinate attachments

A second question implicit in the same meditation is this: Which are the more explosive liberating forces, alternatively, which allow us to neutralise the effects of inordinate attachments in order to arrive at the correct choice? The answer which the meditation gives is that the positive explosive forces are the opposite ones: renouncing having more, being more, renouncing more power, following Christ's example, who became rich by stripping himself of all this. Therefore, this meditation has a place at any moment when, in the clarity of unmasking inordinate attachments, it is about making a correct choice free from their constricting and obsessive function.

Instead, the meditation we have made on Genesis 22 – similar, in my view, but you may not see a similarity there – is located at a level which transcends the experience of individual inordinate attachments in order to go to the root of the victory of faith. And then the question is this: What is the transcendent, fundamental, basic impediment hindering the Christian victory? In other words: in the first part of the meditation on the Two Standards, if we had to imagine what Satan whispers in Abraham's ear while slowly climbing Mount Moriah, the words would be: don't trust this, Abraham, keep what you have. You have something in hand that represents the pledge of God's promise, and this promise binds God, so don't trust him. And what would Satan suggest to us? At this point, given the difficulty prayer can so often present – I mean prolonged prayer of the kind typical during the *Exercises* – I would like to briefly explain two thoughts on this kind of prayer.

Persevering in prolonged prayer

The first thought is a very simple one: prolonged prayer is difficult. St Ignatius tells us this among other things in his thirteenth observation: 'We must remember that during the time of consolation it is easy, and requires only a slight effort, to continue a whole hour in contemplation, but in time of desolation it is very difficult to do so. Hence, in order to fight against the desolation, and conquer the temptation, the exercitant must always remain in the exercise a little more that the full hour. Thus he will accustom himself not only to resist the enemy, but even to overthrow him.' [13]

This way of expressing himself, typical of Ignatius' way of tackling problems, lets us see how of itself, perseverance in prayer is difficult without special help which fundamentally can be outside aid or the internal aid of consolation. It is difficult for reasons we know: aridity, feeling we are in the desert, emptiness, the subject matter doesn't touch me, says nothing to me, so I digress here and there, looking for something to move me and do not find it. It is difficult due to the desolation which is the absence of a sense of God, God is far from me, there is a wall between me and God. Prayer says nothing to me, I feel nothing, I have no desire to do it and feel led to the opposite. Then comes the third difficulty – a result of the second but better separately named: repugnance, rejection of prayer.

It seems to me that these three difficulties show up every time we set ourselves to lengthy prayer, and do not show themselves when we do not. Here, then, lies the temptation not to do it just in order to avoid this problem. Experience, instead, teaches us that it is only in these difficulties that we succeed in understanding what it means to turn to God in a colloquy which truly involves us at depth.

This is the victory of faith in prayer which we need to ask God for in prayer, because it is so difficult, indeed impossible to pursue it alone, insofar as it presumes faith which is God's gift alone. This is the first thought: prolonged prayer is difficult and we have to expect these difficulties and know they will occur.

'Entering into' prayer: a) the 'confessio laudis'

The second thought I explain thus: we need to 'enter into' prolonged prayer. St Ignatius often employs this phrase, 'entering into prayer'. It seems to me that this means that in contrast to shorter prayer which can be spontaneous, easy, immediate, prolonged prayer most often requires us to find the right door to enter. It can happen that we wander about at length, with effort, even if this is meritorious, but cannot enter. So it is important for each of us to find the entrance. As we know, authors of ascetics provide many pointers on how to find it. I would like to recall just two which I feel are important, among the many that books on ascetics suggest.

The first is this: that from the outset we place ourselves before God in our true position, sometimes saying a Psalm, a passage from the Gospel, from Paul, the Prophets; a beginning I would call the *confessio laudis*. This *confessio laudis* is none other than an application of the penitential colloquy to this initial moment, meaning the first point of the general examination of conscience: '*gratias agere Deo pro beneficiis.*' It seems important to me if we truly want to establish who we are, before the Church, before God, first of all to thank God for all the good he has done in us. And I would say not to be too generic: creation, the gift of life, specific gifts over these days, weeks, this month, which have been a certain sign for me of God's goodness, his gift experienced; things that have gone well for me for which I can thank him; things I feel I must thank God for at this moment.

It is already a first panoramic description of who we are before God. We are full of gratitude for many things. So we begin to trust deeply, we cast out into the deep.

Some words, now, on another point of the *Exercises*: the advice '*ad emendandam et reformandam propriam vitam et statum*' [189], for the amendment and reformation of one's way of living, which St Ignatius has follow on from the choice of a state of life properly so called. He says: 'It must be borne in mind that some may be established in an ecclesiastical office, or may be married and hence cannot make a choice of a state of life or, in matter that may be changed and hence are subject to a choice, they may not be very willing to make one. It will be very profitable for such persons… in place of a choice, to propose a way for each to reform his manner of living in his state.'

These are described very briefly with some particular examples. In substance, we are asked 'to desire and seek nothing except the greater praise and glory of God our Lord.' In other words, a choice which excludes situations of discomfort, embarrassment, which in turn are sources of sin. It is not necessary to work out exactly where the fault does or does not lie. It is important and sufficient for a situation to weigh on me, that I experience it as a certain holding back before God that does not leave me free. This dislike, this situation I dare not confront, this somewhat onerous duty I delay in performing will not be formal sinfulness but it displeases me, creates a sense of uneasiness for me; I do not feel I am free before God, so I express my situation before him as it is. This is followed by the second indication: the '*confessio fidei*'.

b) the '*confessio fidei*'

What is the *confessio fidei*? It is the immediate preparation for receiving the word and God's help. That is, I believe, Lord, that your power saves me. I believe, Lord, that the power of Christ who died and rose comes to me to save me from these negative and heavy situations which I know not how to escape. There are sinful situations and we know well how we should act, but there are also difficult, heavy situations which can turn into resistance to God, and just at that moment we do not know how to free ourselves. For example, there are dislikes which weigh heavily on us and which we cannot escape from, so we put them before God. You, Lord, will free me. I cannot remove these things.

This is the *confessio fidei* of someone who looks back over his fragile life before the saving power of God and, in the sacrament of penance, calls on the grace of the Church in his weakness, for forgiveness of formal sins, for the purification of those things that are close to being sinful even if not truly blameworthy, for freedom from those heavy things which prevent us from running to God. Hence, it is clear: the sacrament of penance becomes a 'penitential colloquy'. It carries on a little longer. Instead of lasting three minutes it might last ten, twenty minutes, half an hour or an hour. But I believe it is very restorative for the spirit, especially if helped by someone who perhaps knows us, can put some questions to us, give us some pointers. So, by putting ourselves before God in full freedom, our fears, unease, suffering, moments of repugnance are expressed and clarified in the light of God's mercy.

Penitential spirit and community life

Finally, one last point: the relationship between penance and the penitential spirit, and community life. Here I would like to recall a chapter from Rodriquez' famous *Treatise on Perfection and Christian Virtues*, on accusing ourselves of our sins in the community. I don't recall the exact title, but it was a commentary on the 10th rule of the summary where it says that each person should be 'content with being corrected by the others and helping to correct others' so his faults may be made manifest and be the object of recovery and penance for the community. I was struck by this chapter, because in reading it I noted that really many of the situations which hinder, hold back and block community life would be resolved were there this readiness to recognise our own weaknesses, our fragility, and to recognise those of others, then offer and receive forgiveness.

The true community is one where forgiveness of sins happens: 'Forgive us our trespasses as we forgive those who trespass against us.' It is not a community in which everyone is perfect, not one where the other does what is right and just, and we must demand that of him, but one in which I forgive the other who does not do things well, and also because others will need to forgive me. There is an important relationship, I believe, between a community life in which people easily forgive one another, where penitential practice is more spontaneous, more serene, freer, and a certain transparency of community life. It is something fundamental without which a Christian community cannot exist. The Christian community is a community of individuals who forgive one another daily because they know they are fragile and know they can count on the understanding of others' fragility. It is not necessarily a community of perfect individuals but one of people who learn every day from the forgiveness they receive from God, to forgive others from the bottom of their heart.

This seems to me to be a very important element of community life also because, despite our efforts, we have invincible defects, unconscious kinds of slightly deviant ways of behaving which we will never recover from because they are instinctive and come out before we notice them. Others notice them immediately, but we do so much later and struggle to admit them. Therefore, only a community where forgiveness holds pride of place can see that all its members – all of us – find some breathing space, feel welcome, even when there is something a little less positive about them, and where its member gladly welcome others. It seems to me that there are important relationships between penitential spirit and promoting a true Christian community. It is not something idyllic, not an ideal place, but a place with real people who forgive one another for their faults, their weaknesses and then help one another together to grow in faith and love.

Third Instruction
Qoheleth (the Teacher), Gospel joy, The Rosary

Who is Qoheleth? What does he represent? Clearly, at least for us, he represents the type of disembodied wisdom which is not actually sceptical, I would say, but it does lean toward an elegant skepticism which enables him to rise above human vicissitudes with a kind of smile, knowing that there is not too much cause for hope. To quote an example at random, here is a typical line: 'What is crooked cannot be made straight, and what is lacking cannot be counted' (Ecc 1:15). For sure, with lines like that, not much progress can be made. On the other hand, it is also true that if something just isn't there, it is futile to make plans with it. If something is crooked, how can it be straightened?

Another line comes to me, after reflecting on two *coup d'états* which recently took place in an African nation one after the other; the second one by a non-commissioned officer who had been imprisoned, and once out, took over and gained control of everything. So I open Ecclesiastes and find what Qoheleth wrote: 'Better is a poor but wise youth than an old but foolish king, who will no longer take advice. One can indeed come out of prison to reign, even though born poor in the kingdom.' Then it describes the situation: 'I saw all the living who, moving about under the sun, follow that youth who replaced the king; there was no end to all those people who he led.' Then the Teacher continues: 'Yet those who come later will not rejoice in him' (vv. 15-16). Here is a way of judging human events. It seems that anything can happen but we know how it will end up.

Bitterness, but within a perspective of hope

And so it is with other comments, some more bitter and harsher: 'the same fate comes to all, to the righteous and the wicked, to the good and the evil, to the clean and the unclean, to those who sacrifice and to those who do not sacrifice' (9:2). Things are much the same across the board: 'whether it is love or hate one does not know. Everything that confronts them is vanity' (9:1).

But every now and then in the book we come across lines that we all know: 'All is vanity, except to love and serve God' (*Imitation of Christ*, I, 1), which straightens up the boat a bit and lets us see that behind all this pessimism lies a religious wisdom which helps the reader emerge from it. For example, after the sarcastic and bitter description of old age in Chapter 12, which is really quite dramatic in its bitterness, after 12:12, 'Of making many books there is no end, and much study is a weariness of the flesh,' the conclusion to the whole discourse with which the book also ends, says: 'Fear God and keep his commandments; for that is the whole duty of everyone' (12:13). Clearly, everything here is saved, from a perspective which ultimately trusts in Providence.

A certain balance is gained and emerges, too, within the book, even in passages of a bitter kind that are most beautiful, enjoyable and are more often remembered and make an impression. I like this book very much. It is one I feel so attracted to. We can read it, happily re-read it and enjoy it for its diction, like music or poetry.

In context, though, the book has a broader significance because, written at the end of the Old Testament, it represents the poverty of human effort, even the best of it, faced with the merciful power of God which changes everything. It is like the highest negative preparation for the gospel message. The human being can do very little, has so little to hope for, but then comes the gospel which creates, makes everything new. In this biblical context Ecclesiastes, the Teacher, is like the weariness of the sage who puts down all the books he has written, mostly holy books (and maybe here there is a degree of criticism of all these scrolls) and says; they are useful, but... only if we listen to the word of God: John the Baptist, Jesus who proclaims that the Kingdom is near. Here we have the real anticlimax of the book, which in some respects seems to be the closest to the manifestation of the revelation of God's power and the Lord's newness of life.

Jesus is more radically pessimistic

What can we say about this book in the light of the New Testament? Placing ourselves in the context of the kerygma, Jesus' word, I say that this book is *too little* pessimistic, that it represents a pessimism which is still too subtle, too elegant, too refined. It is the pessimism of someone who is not afraid of himself, can laugh at himself and others, because ultimately he is sure of a degree of balance. Instead, Jesus' pessimism is much more bitter: 'you faithless and perverse generation, how much longer must I be with you? How much longer must I put up with you!'

Therefore, if we take Jesus' expressions – not to mention John the Baptist's: 'You brood of vipers! Who warned you to flee from the wrath to come?' – for example, his tart words in John 6:26: 'You are looking for me, not because you saw signs, but because you ate your fill of the loaves,' we see that Jesus' pessimism is much more radical, rigorous, profound than the Teacher's. At the end, the Teacher balances his pessimism, while Jesus throws it off-balance. It is because of this pessimism regarding humankind that he is called to suffer all its consequences in his body. Like the Teacher, he experiences not only the dullness, childishness, dishonesty of human beings and their inability to produce great projects, but their wickedness, pettiness and cruelty too. The pessimism of Jesus' cry on the cross: 'My God, my God, why have you forsaken me?' (Mt 27:46) goes beyond the Teacher's pessimism. It is such a drastic condemnation of the human condition abandoned by God, which the Teacher would not have dared to say.

Why not? How come Qoheleth continues with his elegant, subtle criticism of self and others which he then balances out? Because clearly his hope was a small hope, so his critique was a small critique: the two correspond. It is the grand critique which creates fear and throws us off-balance because it does not have an equivalent hope and is totally closed to all hope. We all like to laugh, laugh at ourselves a bit, so long as we can keep it all in balance. But immediate, swift censure is launched against humorous critique, protest aimed at ourselves or others which risks compromising this balance, and creates fear and frightens us.

Tolerable limits of pessimism

Ecclesiastes' style of cultured, elegant pessimism cannot exist in the face of great censure which truly calls the individual, situation or status into question. Instead, Jesus can unsettle things to the point of throwing them off-balance, accepting that he is overwhelmed by bitterness and pessimism, inasmuch as he brings with him an infinite hope, the very hope of God in him. Thus he can descend into the depths, can drink the chalice of human pessimism to its dregs, to the last drop, precisely because the fullness of God's hope resides in him.

I believe we can apply this to ourselves as individuals and as a group. As individuals we can arrive at a true self-criticism and also accept the less kind criticisms of others, the harsher ones, to the extent that we can counterbalance them with the compensation of hope, faith, God's power. Otherwise it is logical that we defend ourselves, because our inner balance is involved. There is a certain level of criticism that no one puts up with – if it disturbs his sense of equilibrium, he projects it onto someone else. The same phenomenon happens as a group. It is possible – I speak of an abstract possibility – that a group can carry out self-criticism, nurture a degree of veiled pessimism, but not to the extent of ultimate, fundamental problems. I experience this in myself, for example, when I am faced with some kinds of criticism of myself or our group (criticisms, we could say, of Qoheleth's kind, slightly pessimistic, not much confidence that things can change) where a touch of humour is involved somewhere between the serious and the ridiculous. We can contain this to some extent. But when it goes beyond this and I become the object of violent criticism, I immediately feel myself saying 'enough!' or I immediately think of arguments to the contrary: 'No, it's not like this, you don't know.' In other words, I silence the one telling me.

However, I believe that as we gradually grow in hope we become more able to listen to a certain kind of criticism or to question ourselves, not to turn things inside out, because this is impossible and is not something we do, but because a greater degree of hope allows us to judge ourselves with greater realism than the pessimism that comes from our being human, from things around us. Gospel joy is not a problem of cheerfulness and serenity: it is the ability to pass through all degrees of human suffering with the hope that Christ, who went to the ultimate degree, bears within himself, even though at one point it looked as if he no longer did so, and here we touch on the mystery that is his passion.

Summing up: to a small hope there corresponds an ability to accept minor criticisms, and to great hope there corresponds the ability to accept major criticisms, know how to evaluate them in freedom, joy, and not to immediately defend ourselves or react with swift counter-defence. The latter simply shows that such criticisms, true or false though they may be, have touched on our survival mechanisms and are not balanced by enough hope to bring things back into balance.

This is one reflection of mine to help us explore what we are meditating on: the effects of the kerygma, the joy of the gospel.

I would like to add a brief instruction here that might surprise you. It is on a very simple topic, a very modest and familiar one, but I think it is of some importance.

The Rosary

One aid for a loving contemplation of the mysteries of the Lord's life in an atmosphere of meditative, profound prayer is the rosary. We are all aware that we are in a time when this prayer is falling into disuse, even though not as seriously as is the case for penance. It is a practice that can be replaced by many others. Just the same, it can be interesting to reflect on why this practice has had such influence over the centuries in the West.

I begin with an initial observation: the rosary is not an easy prayer and I believe the error made is to say that it is an easy way of praying when we are tired, when not too much effort is required. For me it has happened that when I have thought of it this way as a prayer for weary moments when we don't know how to pray, it became a bit like a closet, holding all the day's distractions: during my evening rosary these burgeoned instinctively and everything I had done or had to do came to mind. At a certain point I told myself: if this is how things are, then I should let go of the rosary, pick up my diary and look at what I've done or still have to do. That seemed more logical to me until, that is, I reflected a little more and realised that the rosary demands greater presence.

Like the 'Jesus' prayer

There is no doubt that it is a prayer for simple souls, a good prayer for everyone and in this sense an easy prayer. But it is not a prayer that can be said among distractions, even though some seem to be able to pray it well this way. I cannot, so I made a second observation: what is the rosary? I would say that it is the Western version of a prayer the East calls the 'Jesus' prayer. In other words, we have tried to codify this Eastern prayer which I would very simply describe as an internalising of the mystery of Christ through the loving repetition of a simple formula. The simple Eastern formula is this: 'Jesus Christ, son of God, have mercy on me, a sinner.' It can be said by using all four terms in a quaternary rhythm, or also with variations, repeating it many times until it passes from the mind into the heart. It is certainly a prayer with a great history of its own that has had a huge influence as we know from the book: *The Story of a Russian Pilgrim*. There is an entire literature devoted to this prayer.

The Western prayer is rather complex and perhaps it is this that creates difficulties. The *Hail Mary* has ten parts, not four, and so is longer and requires a more concise approach. Maybe this is why it does not have the advantages of the Eastern Jesus prayer, even if its structure, inasmuch as it is repetitive, has Jesus' name at its core, framed by a Gospel episode, and includes an invocation for us sinners, referring to both the present and the final, eschatological moment. The present moment is also considered eschatological: we are always at the hour of death, faced with this fullness of God's judgement which stands over us and is anticipated in this prayer. It really is a very rich formula, perhaps too much so, and therefore may not have the influence, the internalising capacity that the simpler Eastern prayer has.

The rosary 'reduced'

Many other things could be said. I would offer a little suggestion which helps me and could also help others. I told myself: if the Eastern Jesus prayer has no more than three or four elements arranged rhythmically, why could I not say the rosary using a reduced formula of three or four elements, saying it in a calm, tranquil situation, one of recollection, setting in motion a kind of meditation which internalises a mystery from Jesus' life by repeating this brief formula. I find it useful to make a choice of the sentences in the *Hail Mary*, for example, saying just 'full of grace, pray for us' ten times. And saying 'blessed is the fruit of your womb,

Jesus' ten times, repeating it very slowly. Meanwhile, the mystery develops and the internalising takes place. I would do the same where the *Our Father* is concerned, which I find easy to reduce to a simple formula: 'Your kingdom come' or 'forgive us our trespasses', or again, 'do not lead us into temptation.' Here is an internalising which can assist reflection by focusing on the mystery. It could be that doing this also brings with it the desire to extend the formula. But what is essential is to make use of these external aids as the Spirit moves, which the tradition has used over centuries and which have brought so many individuals to deep contemplative prayer. It is a prayer that, among other things, has a mysterious power of inwardly healing the spirit, putting it back in order just as the Jesus prayer from the East does.

So, here is a brief pointer on a prayer that in union with Mary can help us penetrate the mysteries of Jesus' life.

Fourth Instruction
Discernment of spirits

We have reached a stage in the retreat when we begin to pull together a bit the various inner movements (desires, resolutions, proposals, plans), to evaluate them in view of what St Ignatius calls 'the reformation of life'. It can also be very simple, but it should come from a certain connection and resonance with what is going on in us as we gradually meditate and pray.

St Ignatius presumes that we continue with the ordinary meditations but that at a certain point the idea of particular choices is introduced, or a clearer awareness of things emerges in us: directions to foster, decisions to take, things to change.

Discernment of spirits

Two things occur and are practised in all this: a discernment of spirits and a decision-making process. I would like to briefly speak about the first of these by way of comment, and as an encouragement to read the rules for discernment of spirits [313-336].

Since I want to provide a broader panorama for this instruction, I should call it 'Discernment of spirits: Rules for thinking in the Church, Decision-making process.' They are three things which, in my view, could well be considered together. Regarding the second topic, I stress that it deals with rules for thinking *in,* not *with,* the Church as it is usually put. They are not rules for thinking with the Church or the hierarchy, but rules for thinking in truth, for having the right and deep feeling, the precise sense of things in the Church.

I will touch on just a few points regarding this discernment, which are close to my heart and which perhaps I feel inwardly more strongly about because so much is said about them, everyone emphasising one or other point. I might be a bit minimalist in what I say.

What is discernment? Discernment is not decision. One often says: I have made a discernment, to mean, I have decided. This is the wrong way to put it. Discernment is something else altogether which of itself has nothing to do with decision. One can make discernment without any decision. They are two totally different things and we can only see how they come together at a certain moment. When someone says 'I have made a discernment' to mean 'I have decided because I felt this way', it is a caricature of discernment.

The definition I offer is a bit too long and complicated but maybe it expresses well what I want to say: 'Discernment is a prudent judgement on our religious attachment inasmuch as it is a tool and place for bodily mediation of invisible grace'. It is a rather controversial definition which maybe does not say everything that should be said, so let me explain.

INSTRUCTIONS

Evaluation at the level of religious attachment

Discernment is a judgement, an evaluation, an evaluative awareness. Hence it is not a choice, not a decision. In fact, St Ignatius says: '*Regulae ad sentiendum et ad cognoscendum aliquomodo*', 'rules for understanding to some extent... and for recognising...' (313), (Note St Ignatius' delicate approach) and since we are thus sensitised, we can then evaluate things.

Discernment, then, is a certain evaluative understanding made in view of action, even if the action is immediate, that is, the action, as St Ignatius says, of admitting 'good movements produced in the soul' and rejecting the bad ones. So it remains at the level I have called 'religious attachment' about which discernment seeks to somehow provide a 'prudent judgement', a judgement based on a certain reflection and not infallible experience. It is a way of trying to understand this attachment with sincere desire, but with a degree of approximation. I said 'prudent judgement' on our 'religious attachment'. Perhaps the area where discernment operates is determined narrowly here, but we are taking the term 'religious attachment' in a very broad sense, what St Ignatius calls the movements produced in the soul in our relationship with God.

Concerning the emotional resonance of faith

The object of discernment is an emotional movement, meaning our bodily reaction to our cognitive and volitional religious processes. By saying 'religious attachment', I am saying that discernment does not touch on the intimacy of faith which remains secret in God. We are not making discernment on faith, hope or charity, but only on the emotional, bodily resonances integrated within a living, concrete individual, to things that begin from the invisible, untouchable mystery accessible only to God's gaze which addresses faith, hope and charity deep within the human being. Of itself, discernment does not directly touch the interior nature of faith, but its expression in movements of affection which can be very rich: desires, affections, impulses, feeling, emotions, everything that belongs to this area of the cognitive, affective interiority integrated within a living person.

All these movements, forever connected with our bodiliness in some way, can either be a positive or negative sign: positive, hence bearers of joy, peace, consolation, enthusiasm, comfort, rapture, the desire to do something, give ourselves to everyone, throw ourselves into something, martyrdom etc. Or negative, hence repulsion, disgust, anger, resentment, sense of distance from everything the divine world represents or reminds us of etc. In other words, the whole gamut of emotional resonance and this in a broad sense, be it cognitive or volitional, positive or negative.

To see if they come from grace

In the attempt I made to define discernment, in order to encourage response from different view points, I said it is a "prudent judgement" on these emotional resonances, to see which are to be nurtured and encouraged, which are to be removed and rejected so we can know how to regulate ourselves in this varied and tumultuous world which is the great cauldron of our religious attachment. Naturally, one understands, the point of reference and arrival for this prudent judgement of our religious attachment is the 'invisible grace', the gift of faith, the presence of the Spirit at work. This Spirit, received through all this ebullience or lack of it, moves in the bodily life of the concrete individual.

However, a very delicate problem arises here that could make this discernment of spirits a risky or difficult tool to make use of. All the interior movements I have described – impulses, feelings, emotions, or fears, disgust, repulsion etc. – are submitted not only to the intimate factor of faith that takes bodily form but also to many other different factors coming more from the outside, even if mostly internal to us, which we call moods, health, digestion, time, circumstances that bother us, anything which in any way represents an event that tries to insert itself into our psyche and determine it in some way. Hence the difficulty of truly discerning what is an inner movement that faith allows us to lead to the action of the transforming God in us, from what is simply an expression of our vitality – the air round here is fresh, we can breathe well and are content, we begin to pray joyfully, all is well, because there is this outward vitality.

It is true that from a providential outlook this could all be called a gift of God, and so we can enter into discernment in a broad sense. But if we feel we are much affected by moods or other external factors, it is not the world of religious attachment as such that is aroused from deep within the person. It is what counts in particular for negative moods. One can be in the worst of moods but be under the profound influence of grace, if the bad mood is due to external circumstances such as when we have a headache, or find ourselves in a different situation, and these things mean that psychologically we are not able to properly receive the influence of grace. Nevertheless, the person experiences this reality profoundly.

A first conclusion comes from this attempt at a definition. As we can understand from St Ignatius' incisive 'to some extent', discernment requires us to be very self-possessed. When someone says: 'God wants this from me' or 'The Lord has made me understand that...' I say to myself, how does he know that? Just as well he understands, I don't find it easy to understand these things. I say 'just as well', situating comments like these in an atmosphere of faith, Providence. But when they are linked with certain desires, anxieties, enthusiasm, my first reaction is to be a bit distrustful. We are not able to immediately arrive at statements like this. It is wonderful to get to that point, and we do, in due course, but they cannot be our first quick conclusion.

Two principles for right discernment

Discernment of spirits is not easy. It is not something mechanical, something that can be applied mathematically. So on what principles is discernment based? In my view, it is based on two fundamental principles with very profound theological and biblical roots. The first is this: God wants to lead us to salvation, in view of which, God is at work in the world, in history and also in me. But what is salvation? Salvation is the *shalom*, as the Scriptures say, the fullness of times, of positivity, joy, peace, serenity, happiness. Hence, it is clear that God's action is tangentially along these lines, so joy, peace, happiness, enthusiasm, serenity are, in the end, criteria for discerning divine activity. But by saying 'in the end', I mean that there could be some anxious and difficult moments. Look at the discernment Abraham had to go through to understand that he did not have to carry through with the killing of his son! A discernment not of joy, peace, tranquility but of tremendous anxiety, violent engagement. Hence the rule applies, but in terms of its eschatological finality, open to the kingdom of God. This can be applied to other circumstances but with due prudence and attention.

To this first theological principle – that God wants to lead us to salvation, to *shalom*, fullness of joy, peace, the messianic goods and to be able to appreciate this at depth – I would add a second: God is at work within me, '*intimior intimo meo*'; at work in an invisible, imperceptible but very real way, because just as he recreates me as a person through his constant action, so does he recreate me as his son through an equally constant action which is the root of all that is achieved in me in the area of faith, hope and charity.

This action of God's is the basis of everything we can say about ourselves in Christian life. From this action of the Father's in giving me the Son, and the action of the Son in giving me the Spirit, and of the Spirit in forming the Son in me and handing me over to the Father; from this action that forms my most intimate Christian personality and from which all the rest flows; from this invisible, untouchable, unverifiable object of faith alone and gift received in faith, comes an inner energy, the mysterious energy of faith which radiates through the person.

This radiance can be grasped at a certain point, and it is here that it seems to me the discernment of spirits takes place: in grasping the radiance of faith, or rather, not faith itself but as it radiates in us.

All the Ignatian rules of discernment of spirits involving consolation and desolation should lead back to these elements. They are the various applications, very important pieces of advice, the more precise psychological indicators of these two fundamental principles. Yet, they are insufficient. There is a third element without which these two are not yet well calibrated and can even lead to wild discernment from which we begin to think, well, who knows what we might begin to think. But the things that do emerge at this point are things that are not so important.

The third element in this: God not only works '*intimior intimo meo*' in creating me as a subject of faith, hope and charity, but he builds up a new world in Christ. I accept God's commitment to the new Covenant of building this new world, in faith as a gift, as promise. And this construction of a new world in Christ must also be part of the discernment.

FIFTH INSTRUCTION
The *Exercises* and daily life

I now come to a reflection that could seem a little like one of Qoheleth's ideas, a rather pessimistic one. Nevertheless, it is something I feel very much and it seems useful to present it. What is the real connection between the *Exercises* and daily life?

What is the principal difference between the *Exercises* – the communion of life that goes on in them through Eucharist, being together, personal exchange etc. – and community life which seeks to reproduce this climate of the *Exercises* in some way?

To me it seems we err sometimes when we think that this climate can become a model which we then transfer to daily life. It amazes us that people who have prayed so well together find themselves so divided, with different ideas, at odds, in daily life. But this division is normal and I would like to explain why. The reason is that transcendent values, fundamental choices at the level of the theological virtues, are at play in the *Exercises*. Mediations are all short-term ones and people go immediately to final realities, those on which agreement is easier, and common feeling more rapidly achieved. There is a climate of prolonged prayer, silence, calm and this leads to the gradual emergence of unity and communion around these grand, final values.

Ultimate and more immediate values

In everyday life, instead, it is the immediate, indirect values that are in play. Long-term mediations, the transcendent end, the victory of faith come about through and at the end of a long series of particular, concrete mediations subject to a specificity that does not submit to the laws of the religious dynamic but to the laws which pertain to the ordinary dynamic of daily matters. What prevails in daily life is the area belonging to the cardinal virtues – prudence, justice, fortitude, temperance – with all the attendant attitudes: communication, dialogue, courtesy, good administration, punctuality, order, logic, efficiency etc.

Now it is clear that communion is easier while we are in the area of the theological virtues, when we go not to theological discussions but to prayer, basic values, values of the mystery. By contrast, in the practical arena, conflicts and misunderstandings are much more frequent because the problems are more specific, even when there are people of good will who maybe pray together and agree on transcendent choices. It is clear, normal that this be so, and it is to be expected. That does not mean that the retreat has not been well made or that understanding achieved on transcendent values was false. Rather does it mean that the two areas are distinct.

We cannot extrapolate a certain fusion of souls at the level of faith, hope and charity, to then ignore problems dividing us due to so many different ways things can be done. We need to resolve matters according to reason, measure and the criteria for doing and resolving these things. What we call misunderstandings, community differences, different outlooks and tensions which may arise are, so to speak, the daily bread of life in common and are to be accepted as such. Nor do we need to think that we create community by eliminating them, because that will never be the case. What creates community is forgiveness for misunderstandings repeatedly expected and offered; it is humble and open dialogue on the different ways of acting. These very community crises ought contribute to creating this community. We should not confuse the two orders. The fact that we agree on the superior order which is certainly very beautiful, does not eliminate conflict or somehow prevent us from treading on someone's toes. It is impossible to live together without this happening sometimes. We need to accept it as one side of life in common.

An enlightening comparison

One thing Fr Godin said about today's Pentecostal communities struck me. When he was asked for some conclusions of a sociological nature on these communities (and I have much respect for them because I am partly involved and do not want to criticise them with these comments) he observed that two things are noted: on the one hand, an apparent 'unanimity in the alleluias' they constantly cry, and on the other, strong conflict. Perhaps there are no conflicts as powerful as those in Pentecostal communities, despite them being specialists in embrace, joy, singing alleluia, etc. According to Fr Godin, this exists in fact and comes out at a certain point. It would be strange if that were not the case. Some people are scandalised: How come? These communities talk so much about love and fellowship and here they are, divided over matters of prestige, or the direction this or some other group has taken, who has rights, etc. These things happen. It is just the confusion of the two orders that causes us to be scandalised. We have to say that this is why the 11th decree insists so much on the two orders, that is, the order of transcendent truths and the order of practice, so that they may influence and benefit each other. It is clear that the order of our retreat, the *Exercises*, as we have experienced it with its focus on promise and faith, provides inspiration, joy, peace in the order of daily life as well, and hence tends to bring conflicts into the ambit of reason, dialogue, common sense, humility, acceptance, practicality that might otherwise be impossible. For its part, the pragmatic order of daily matters removes the risk that the order of the retreat remains only words, proclaimed but not truly incarnated words, light that does not warm, words that do not spread. So the shock of daily life with all its limitations, its apparent pettiness and banality, is needed so that the word which has been contemplated is truly lived in the flesh. There is no other way of living it except in daily life. Therefore, I would conclude as follows:

1. We should not be under any illusions, because daily life is difficult and always will be. It is an inexorable millstone which grinds down many beautiful ideas and beautiful resolutions.

2. Just the same, it would be a mistake to have no hope, because faith conquers the world and the seed of the word ground and broken down bears fruit. It is precisely this grinding and breaking down which the word receives in daily life, with its little experiences of difficulty, incomprehension, things that shouldn't be, unresolved problems, frustrations which leave us feeling anxious, which to me seems to incarnate the seed of the word in everyday reality, and allows us to feel the strength, the power of this word.

Let us pray for one another, then, and for others, so we can truly experience the power of God's word in daily life.

CARLO MARIA MARTINI Foundation

The Carlo Maria Martini Foundation came into existence through the initiative of the Italian Province of the Jesuits and with the involvement of the Archdiocese of Milan.

It aims at remembering Cardinal Carlo Maria Martini by promoting knowledge and study of his life and works and keeping alive the spirit that animated his commitment, encouraging experience and knowledge of the Word of God in the context of our contemporary culture.

With this in mind, the Foundation's role is spelt out in a number of specific actions:

- Bringing the Cardinal's works, writings and addresses together in an archive and promoting their study as well as encouraging and authorising their publication.
- Supporting and nurturing ecumenical and inter-religious dialogue, with civil society and non-believers as well, working closely together to understand the indissoluble connection between faith, justice and culture.
- Fostering the study of Scripture involving other disciplines, including spirituality and social sciences.
- Contributing to pastoral and formative projects valuing Ignatian pedagogy and addressed especially to the young.
- Supporting study of the meaning and extended practice of the Spiritual Exercises.

Those who wish to can contribute to the collection of materials (written, audio, video) on Cardinal Martini by indicating initiatives regarding him by writing to segretaria@fondazionecarlomariamartini.it

To subscribe to the newsletter (in Italian) and support the Foundation's activities: www.fondazionecarlomariamartini.it

BIBLICAL MEDITATIONS

A selection of sermons, retreats and meditation texts drawn from the vast work of Cardinal Martini. There is a roundup of biblical personalities from Old and New Testaments, explanations, some chosen topics to accompany reflections on the human being in search of God. The inestimable legacy of a man of prayer and contemporary spirituality.

1. **The Accounts of the Passion.** Meditations
2. **Paul.** In the thick of his ministry
3. **Our Father.** Do not heap up empty phrases
4. **The Apostles.** Men of peace and reconciliation
5. **Abraham.** Our father in faith
6. **Jesus.** Why he spoke in parables?
7. **Elijah.** The living God
8. **Stephen.** Servant and witness
9. **Peter.** Confessions
10. **Jacob.** A man's dream
11. **Jeremiah.** A prophetic voice in the city
12. **Israel.** A people on the move
13. **Samuel.** Religious and civil prophet
14. **Timothy.** Timothy's way

www.ingramcontent.com/pod-product-compliance
Lightning Source LLC
Chambersburg PA
CBHW030635150426
42811CB00077B/2111/J